INTREPID AFRICA

Mark Elliott
Anna Rockall
Matt Rudd
Ed Waller
Mark Eveleigh
Juliet Coombe
Nikita Gulhane
Chris Caldicott
Sharon Harris
Geoff Crowther
Colin Field
Liz Durno
Steve Davey
Graham Boynton
Chris Bradley
Jon Ronson

Edited by: Ian Jackson & Liz Edwards

la belle aurore

First published in the United Kingdom in 2001 by

La Belle Aurore
15 Ballater Road
London SW2 5QS
Tel: 020-7924 0856
www.labelleaurore.com

Intrepid Africa © La Belle Aurore 2001

ISBN 0 9534423 2 2

Editor: Ian Jackson

Sub-editor: Liz Edwards

Concept and Finance: Juliet Coombe, La Belle Aurore

Production and Design: Steve Davey, La Belle Aurore

Cover photography: Steve Davey, La Belle Aurore

Contents

COUNTRIES OF INTREPID AFRICA

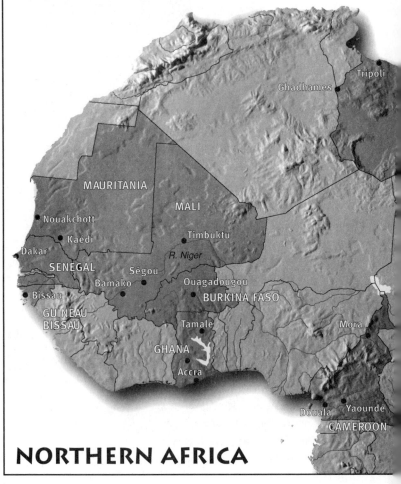

Tripoli

Ghadhames

MAURITANIA

MALI

Nouakchott

Timbuktu

Kaédi

R. Niger

Dakar

SENEGAL

Ségou

Bamako

Ouagadougou

Bissau

BURKINA FASO

GUINEA BISSAU

Tamale

Mora

GHANA

Accra

Douala   Yaoundé

CAMEROON

NORTHERN AFRICA

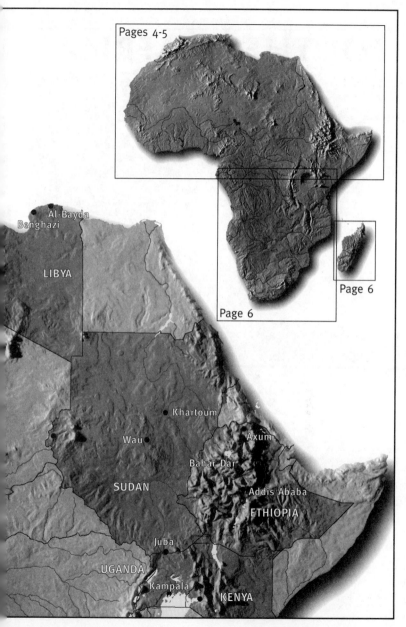

Pages 4-5

Page 6

Page 6

Al-Bayda
Benghazi

LIBYA

Khartoum

Wau

Axum

Bahar Dar

SUDAN

Addis Ababa

ETHIOPIA

Juba

UGANDA

Kampala

KENYA

5

SOUTHERN AFRICA

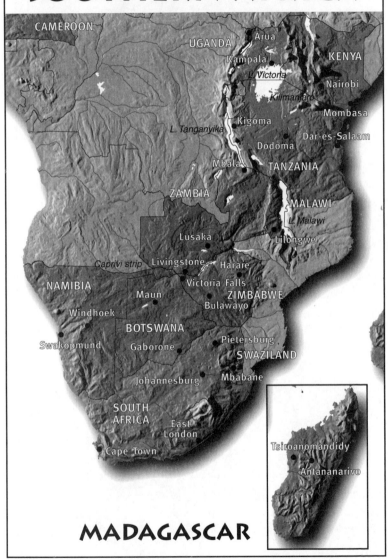

CAMEROON

UGANDA
Arua
Kampala
KENYA
L. Victoria
Nairobi
Kilimanjaro
Mombasa
Kigoma
Dar-es-Salaam
L. Tanganyika
Dodoma
Mbala
TANZANIA
ZAMBIA
MALAWI
L. Malawi
Lusaka
Lilongwe
Caprivi strip
Livingstone
Harare
NAMIBIA
Victoria Falls
Maun
ZIMBABWE
Windhoek
Bulawayo
BOTSWANA
Swakopmund
Pietersburg
Gaborone
SWAZILAND
Johannesburg
Mbabane
SOUTH
AFRICA
East
London
Cape Town
Tsiroanomandidy
Antananarivo

MADAGASCAR

Writers & Editors

Intrepid Africa is the collaboration of a number of writers and editors from around the world.

Ian Jackson

After nine years on Australian newspapers Ian decided it was time to pack it all in and head for London. Following 18 months in South Asia, where he got intimately acquainted with squat bogs and countless strange forms of transport, he arrived in the UK. In London he was travel editor and then editor of *TNT* magazine, the leading magazine for travellers and Australasians. He is now features editor at *Geographical* magazine.

Liz Edwards

A six-month stint as an au-pair in France convinced Liz that getting to know other countries was good, and that having children was bad. Her travels have taken her down the Nile, the Mekong and the Paraguaçu rivers, as well as plenty of trips on dry land. Having rejected a career in the law for a more honourable one in journalism, she moved on from the travel trade press to become Staff Writer at *Wanderlust*, one of the UK's leading travel magazines.

Mark Elliott

Though he prides himself on never going anywhere 'really dangerous' Mark prefers to holiday where there's recently been a coup or 'minor civil unrest'. His books for Trailblazer Publications include the first guide to Azerbaijan and Asia Overland for which he traversed the continent seven times. His African experiences include a five-month spell as a researcher in a Gambian village, interviewing local witch doctors and learning how to make love potions.

Anna Rockall

Anna is a freelance writer, who particularly enjoys writing on active and adventurous travel and culinary exploration. She has jungle-trekked in Sumbawa, galloped over the Rockies, climbed Kilimanjaro, riverboarded down the Zambezi, paraglided over the Alps, dived the Red Sea, and hiked in the Grand Canyon. She has eaten ants in Oaxaca, mopane worms in Zambia, goat in Jamaica and much nicer things too. Her next project is a round-the-world yacht race.

Matt Rudd

Matt isn't proud that his career began by lying to Australian editors about his journalistic credentials. Today, he is Assistant Editor of *Wanderlust*, one of the UK's leading travel magazines, and contributes regularly to BBC London Live. He travels regularly, finding new adventures in Cambodia, Belarus, Azerbaijan and New South Wales. Southern Africa on the other hand is an old favourite thanks to his family's South African and Zimbabwean roots.

Ed Waller

Since first trying his hand at travel writing aged 7¾, with *What I Did On My Holidays*, Ed has learnt backgammon in the souks of Damascus, taught Kurdish kids to juggle, and been trounced at chess by Cossacks on a train from Hong Kong to Calais. This chapter of Ed's life ended up with him mixing cement in Tel Aviv, so it wasn't too long before his trusty rucksack was seeing action in the jungles of South America, the Saudi Arabian deserts and the ice floes of Scandinavia.

Mark Eveleigh

In 1996 Mark Eveleigh FRGS led the first expedition by foreigners into Central Borneo's 'valley of the spirit world' collecting material for his book, *Fever Trees of Borneo*. He grew up in Africa and returned in 1999 to travel through Madagascar. After crossing the north of the island with a zebu 'pack bull' he set out to trek across the bandit country of the Zone Rouge. The full story is told in *Maverick in Madagascar*, published by Lonely Planet in April 2001.

Juliet Coombe

Juliet, co-founder of La Belle Aurore, regularly contributes to newspapers, magazines, guidebooks, internet sites and TV programmes. Her food safaris have included eating roast guinea pig in Ecuador, rat curry in Thailand and green ants bottoms in Australia, which is the Aboriginal cure for flu. She has seen the inside of a Zambian jail, been shot at in a traditional Yemen gun festival and had tea with Sheik Amir, Sheikh Isa bin Salman, Bahrain's ruler since 1961.

Nikita Gulhane

After graduating from university, Nik spent several years working as a geologist on oil rigs in the North Sea, Italy and Gabon. After cheating death by hurricane off the coast of Belize, he realised there was more to life than work and joined BBC Radio. As a presenter and reporter he has visited India, Cuba, Miami, Trinidad and Newcastle. Following a visit to East Greenland he has now entered his 'polar phase' with his sights set on South Georgia and Antarctica.

Chris Caldicott

Following a course in Photographc Arts at the Central London School of Communication, Chris began a life on the road. Between 1991 and 1996 he was Expedition Photographer-in-Residence for the Royal Geographical Society, taking him to Brunei, Badia of Jordan and the Mkomazi Reserve in Tanzania. He now writes and photographs for a variety of publications and is co-owner with his wife Carolyn of the World Food Cafe in Covent Garden, London.

Sharon Harris

Sharon is a freelance writer and guidebook researcher. In 1994, a clairvoyant told her, "You'll do a lot of travelling in your job," before shrieking, "they don't pay you much!" Two months later she embarked on her first flight, to Zimbabwe, where she voluntarily updated the Rough Guide to gain a free book. Years later some European research contracts followed. In 2000 she returned to Africa to battle with wild animals, passport-hunting males and mosquitoes.

Geoff Crowther

Geoff was born and bred in Yorkshire, UK. He now lives in Nairobi, Kenya, with Alice Njoki, a Kikuyu from Kiambu, who keeps his excesses in check. In the meantime, he wrote a stack of Lonely Planet's guidebooks to Africa, South America, India and Asia which sold far too many for comfort and laid him open to criticism from overland companies, African dictators and individual travellers who, referring to them as 'bibles', sometimes took them too literally.

Colin Field

Born in England, Colin grew up in Canada where his interest in bicycles bloomed. At the age of 18 he began travelling with a VW combi and some Grateful Dead tickets, and after years of thumbing and cycling through numerous continents, the wanderlust shows no sign of dying. He is currently living and working at a mountain bike camp in central Canada, where plans for the future change daily. Writing and cycling are the two addictions that remain constant.

Liz Durno

Liz was born in Cape Town, South Africa, where she studied journalism and worked in newspapers before spending a year farming in Zambia. She returned to her hometown of East London, SA to resume her journalistic career before undertaking a belated working holiday and moving to East London in the UK two years ago. Although she is mostly involved in sub-editing and production work now, she retains her passion for writing and travel.

Steve Davey

Writer, photographer and co-founder of La Belle Aurore, Steve has travelled through Africa, Asia and Europe in a quest for the improbable blend of exploration, spirituality and excitement, following the theory that if you aren't in the middle of the action, then you might as well give up and go home. Home is Brixton in London — the closest you can get to travelling without needing your passport — in an eclectic house dominated by a rather large ginger cat.

Graham Boynton

Graham is the Travel Editor of the *Telegraph* and *Sunday Telegraph*. Born in Britain, he grew up in southern Africa, and entered journalism as a political reporter at the height of the Rhodesian war and the heyday of apartheid. In 1976 he was declared an 'undesirable alien' by the South African government and deported. He wrote *Last Days in Cloud Cuckooland*, on the final days of white rule in Africa, one of the *Washington Post*'s Best Books of 1998.

Chris Bradley

Chris spent eight years as a Tour Group leader in Egypt, Jordan, India and Central Asia. He still leads special interest groups. He has written for the Insight Yemen guide, as well as his own Discovery Guide. As a filmmaker, he wrote and produced a documentary on the Shetland Oil Disaster for National Geographic. He lectures at the Royal Geographical Society and contributes to *Wanderlust*, *Trail Walker*, *Arabian Wildlife* and *Mountain Biking UK*.

Jon Ronson

Writer and documentary filmmaker, Jon's work has included the *Human Zoo* column for the *Guardian* and BBC Radio 4 documentary *Hotel Auschwitz*. For Channel 4, Jon has made *Tottenham Ayatollah, New Klan, New York to California (A Great British Odyssey), Dr Paisley, I Presume*, the four-part *Critical Condition* and late-night chat show *For The Love Of...* For BBC2 he made *The Ronson Mission*. His book, *Them: Adventures With Extremists* is published by Picador.

Foreword

by The Publishers

T his book is about travel, and this book is about Africa. Both are often misunderstood, maligned and taken for granted. Travel has become a rite of passage, a filler for the curriculum vitae in a university gap year or a wind-down after working too hard. It is too often seen as something to get out of your system before getting on with the real business of living your life. But for many people, travel is their life. This is the case with the writers on these pages, and this is the spirit with which we bring you Intrepid Africa.

You might not feel adventurous or confident enough to cycle to Timbuktu or to walk across the badlands of Madagascar yourself, but this needn't stop you travelling. Travel is not about hardships or tests of endurance. It is about putting yourself in an unfamiliar situation with an open mind. It is about talking to people and listening to people, whether they be locals or other travellers. It is about experiencing the unfamiliar and learning more about yourself by learning more about other people and places. This can happen when you are riding a train through the desert or a ferry down one of the great lakes of Africa, or it can come when you get down from an overland truck and talk to a group of locals, rather than hiding behind the façade of western superiority.

Travel can be the most demanding and enlightening thing that you ever do. You may well experience hardship, discomfort or regret, but you will feel more alive than you ever have done before, and you will learn and realise things that will change your life and help to shape and guide you in the future.

Many people are worried about travelling, believing it to be risky or dangerous. In a world where walking home at night, crossing the road or even eating beef has worries and dangers, where a third of us will develop cancer at some point in our lives, then travelling is comparatively safe.

Waiting three days for a cancelled flight from Nairobi to Harare, I met a 96-year-old Australian woman who was, as she freely admitted, travelling for the last time. She had been on the road on and off since she was 36 and was on a final tour of the world. She was old and frail and was suffering from a badly broken arm as the result of a mugging back home in Melbourne. She sums up the spirit of our books as much as anyone. She was out there doing it. Living the life. Meeting people, talking to people. Seeing things, and with the urgency that can only come with old age, she was thirsty to experience life. The East Africans called her '*Mama*' and doors that were firmly closed to other travellers were opened to her just because of her age.

Africa is always full of such paradoxes. More than 50 countries jostle for position on a continent that was the birthplace of civilisation. There are hundreds of peoples and languages and a fantastic diversity of cultures and history, yet all we are used to hearing about Africa is wars and famines and disaster.

More than anywhere else on Earth, Africa is all about space, landscapes and culture. It is about great rivers, deserts and plains, and wildlife in concentrations that are unseen anywhere else.

We hope that with this book we will inspire you to travel to Africa, or maybe even bring back a few old memories if you have travelled there before. One thing is for certain. Once you have travelled to Africa it never leaves you. The sights, the sounds, the smells and the majesty will come back to you at the strangest times, whether it be on hearing African voices drifting past on your local high street or seeing a bizarrely shaped fruit at the greengrocers, that you last saw was being waved at you across a crowded market.

Never mind about the checklist of things to take before you travel: the pills and potions, the cameras, book, maps and boots. The most important thing you can ever take to Africa is an open mind — and maybe a sense of humour helps as well.

Introduction

by Martin Roberts

A frica. The word alone conjures up images of travel and adventure. Eight thousand kilometres from the shores of the Mediterranean to the rocky outcrop at the Cape of Good Hope. Thirty million square kilometres of deepest, darkest, tribal-dancing, river-flowing, mountain-climbing, jungle-sweating, road-bumping, hair-braiding, wildlife-watching, people-smiling, desert-shimmering, sea-fishing, wood-carving, friendship-making, beach-baking, mind-blowing possibilities.

But where do you start? Mainstream holiday brochures will tempt you to the tourist hotspots across the continent, but in Africa there's still a chance to practice the ancient art of real travel. Arriving in towns where you will be the only foreign face. Heading along roads where you'll not see another vehicle for hours. Watching the kind of wildlife Sir David Attenborough should be providing a personal commentary on.

I have seen the Big Five. Buffalo sweeping majestically, lions roaring masterfully, elephants charging violently, leopard slinking malevolently, rhino wallowing indulgently. But my favourite thing of all? Better than the whales off the Cape of South Africa. More colourful than the flamingos on the great lakes in Kenya or Tanzania. More breathtaking than the silverback gorillas in Rwanda's Mountains of the Moon. It's a dung beetle. Rolling a massive ball of elephant doo-doos down a dusty track in

Swaziland. We'd been bouncing along in an open-topped Land Rover for three hours and had stopped for a lunch break. I was presenting a story for TV and our cameraman was scanning the scene for potential shots through his telephoto lens. Appearing out of the heat haze on the dirt road, he noticed a 20cm ball, seemingly rolling itself along. We all scuttled over to investigate. Using his front mandible and skipping along on his rear legs, a male dung beetle was pushing what, to us, would have been the equivalent of an eight-metre truffle along the road.

Meanwhile his mate/partner/lover/work colleague sat on the ball enjoying the ride and jiggling around so as not to fall off. We watched, transfixed. After 50m the two beetles exchanged roles and continued their journey from somewhere to heaven knows, down a dust track in the middle of the African bush. They had no real concept of how long the road was or where they could reach if they rolled for long enough. But they were contented with their manageable section of the bigger picture.

A traveller to Africa could learn much from the humble dung beetle. At first the sheer scale of the place can seem daunting. But trying to grasp its vastness is as pointless as the dung beetle worrying that the track it is on continues for another 5,000km, and that it would take umpteen thousand generations of rolling to complete. Instead, all you can realistically hope to do is pick small areas of this wonderland and experience those to the full. And if inspiration is what you need, then you will find it in this book. A captivating selection of stories from across the continent, from Mauritania in the west to Madagascar in the east and down from Libya to southern Africa. Tales that will leave you inspired and motivated.

Mark Elliott grapples with corruption and royal etiquette in Cameroon. Chris Caldicott endures a gruelling overland journey so he can say he's actually been to Timbuktu and witnessed one of the world's most spectacular migrations. Mark Eveleigh encounters magic and supernatural powers in Madagascar and Jon Ronson accidentally finds himself on an overland journey, with a group of brilliantly well-observed fellow travellers. There are many more, varied in content and destination, but similar in the evocative way they bring the continent to life.

I have been lucky enough to experience a lot of what Africa has to offer which is why I can put my hand on my heart and say that it really is a magical place. I've seen the sun rise over the cradle of mankind from the slopes of Kilimanjaro before making the final push to the summit. I have dived with turtles off the beaches near Mombasa. I have drunk fine wines in the vineyards of Stellenbosch. I have plummeted 100m towards the foaming Zambezi, bungee jumping off the bridge that links Zambia to Zimbabwe. I have flown in a microlight over Victoria Falls at sunset, then returned to the falls themselves after dark when the full moon created a black and white moonbow instead of the usual multi-coloured daytime one. I have slept in four-poster beds in five-star hotels and on blankets under the stars. I am, without doubt, in love with the place.

However, there have been moments when we've squabbled. And whilst climbing Kilimanjaro we almost had a major falling out.

I inched slowly forwards, the path lit by moonlight and the beams of head torches. A slow crocodile of amateur adventurers, pushing themselves to the limit of their abilities. One tiny step after another, then a gasping pause to catch a breath as the effects of lack of oxygen at altitude began to increase.

We were on the final leg of our climb to the summit. All that stood between us and victory was a 1,000m struggle up a near-vertical slope of scree and loose rocks, known as the Western Breach. We had been woken up at 11pm and had started climbing at midnight. This was supposedly so that the scree slope would still be frozen and easier to scale, but from the occasional moonlit glimpses of the sheer drops all around, I reckoned the real reason was that we would have freaked out had we seen where we were going.

Eight hours later we were still climbing. It was like being strapped to a StairMaster on cardio workout for a whole day. This was always going to be the hardest part of the ascent, but nothing could have prepared me for the mental and physical struggle we endured that night.

Just as spirits reached their lowest ebb, a faint glimmer of orange appeared on the horizon. Gradually a crimson sun crept upwards, highlighting the tops of billowing clouds below us and illuminating the feeble path we had been creeping along. Moments later its fiery orange rim nudged into view and bathed our faces in warming light. Hearts pounding, we stared in awe at sunrise over Africa and the plains of the Serengeti. It was an incredibly magical and spiritual moment.

Soon after, we took the last few painful steps to the summit and collapsed on each other in emotional celebration. The biggest challenge of our lives, and we had actually done it. We had climbed to the highest point on the African continent, the 5,802m peak of Mount Kilimanjaro, and we'd raised loads of money for a good cause at the same time. Talk about a sense of achievement.

I had chosen to join 24 other adventures on the annual climb of Kilimanjaro which is organised to raise money for the NSPCC. Part of the money for the trip goes straight to the charity and whatever money you can raise on top in sponsorship is a bonus. It's an increasingly popular way of supporting your favourite cause, and having the holiday of a lifetime. The itinerary was a pleasing nine days on the mountain followed by a two-day safari in one of Tanzania's excellent game parks, and four days of relaxation at a beach hotel on the spice island of Zanzibar.

The climb started in lush tropical rainforest on the lower slopes of the mountain. Exotic flowers and creepers drooped over a narrow path as we hiked like characters from an Indiana Jones movie through the dense undergrowth. Porters carried our rucksacks, leaving us with just a lightweight day pack containing water, snacks and extra clothing. They also carried an amazing collection of food and cooking equipment, which they used to rustle together meals of outstanding quality at all but the highest altitudes. They wakened us with early morning tea, created elaborate picnics for lunch and crafted steaming stews and roast chicken dinners at night. Smiling and courteous, they flip-flopped their way up the mountain, massive plastic containers strapped to their heads with string, while we struggled onwards in our Gortex clothing, low-impact boots and other technologically advanced equipment.

On average we walked for five to six hours a day, arriving at camp to find the tents already erected and warm water ready for washing. There was nowhere to plug your hairdryer in, but fresh mountain streams left your hair silky and sweet smelling.

The following days were spent in a happy routine of waking at 6am, eating a hearty breakfast, climbing during the day, relaxing before dinner, playful camaraderie during the evening meal and then lively conversation around a campfire under a blanket of stars.

From rainforest we moved up through areas of giant heather and onto the Shira Plateau — a vast wide plain dotted with everlasting flowers and small trees. Soon after, the effects of the altitude became apparent. Steps became laboured, like walking through treacle and we were soon out of breath. It is possible to do the climb in three days, via the popular and now, rather crowded *Mwengi* or Coca-Cola route, as it has become known, but our seven day wilderness route allowed more time for acclimatisation and therefore a much greater chance of success.

By the time we arrived at our final camp we had reached 5,000m and the scenery had changed to a barren, high altitude desert. Low clouds drifted across a timeless moonscape. Then, as clouds cleared, we stared open-mouthed at our final challenge: that Western Breach.

I will never forget the events of the following night, nor the elation I had on reaching the summit. It is an achievement I will be proud of for the rest of my life and one which gives me strength in all aspects of the things I do now. When a problem occurs I just think, Well, I managed to climb 'Kili', this is nothing in comparison. You don't get that from a fortnight on a beach in Spain.

After such an invigorating but exhausting experience, we were all ready for some serious rest and relaxation. Thankfully Tanzania has a wealth of opportunities for it.

First we headed to Tarangire National Park — tens of thousands of acres of wild African savannah making up one of the country's top game viewing areas. As two baby giraffes scampered across the road, ten metres from one side of our Land Rover, and a huge elephant happily chomped grass five metres from the other, we appreciated why it is regarded as such.

Then we were Zanzibar-bound. Sipping a cocktail overlooking a turquoise ocean from the balcony of our five-star beachfront hotel, it was hard to believe the comparison with where we had been just a few days earlier. But it doesn't take long to get reacquainted to relaxing in the lap of luxury.

The island itself is fascinating to explore. Famous as a trading post for exotic spices like cloves, cinnamon, nutmeg and vanilla, legend has it that Zanzibar was also the home port of Sinbad the Sailor. It was certainly the starting point for colonial explorers such as Livingstone on their journeys into the interior.

Little seems to have changed as you watch white-sailed *dhows* float into the main harbour of Zanzibar Town. In the area known as Stone Town, ramshackle buildings with gnarled wooden-shuttered windows hang over narrow streets, and stalls sell exotic spices and antiques.

Back on the beach, another cocktail in hand, I saluted a fiery orange sun as it slipped into the ocean. I knew there would currently be another group of climbers on Kilimanjaro, eagerly awaiting its return.

This book contains many accounts of similar memorable journeys and experiences, but there is nothing here that you couldn't experience for yourself. The travel may, at times, be arduous. It may not be as packaged as you would like or as air-conditioned as you've come to expect. But it's there, waiting for you. Travel there now through the eyes of our authors, then travel to Africa yourself and let your own adventure unfold.

Martin Roberts is a TV travel presenter, film director, journalist and photographer. He is also chairman of the British Guild of Travel Writers and founder member of the Dung Beetle Appreciation Society.

A brolly good time in Cameroon

by Mark Elliott

C ameroon hits you in the face like a barber with a hot wet towel. Before you know it you're steamed and stifled, and hoping that the chap holding a scalpel to your neck only wants to give you a shave. On arrival I knew only three things about the country. 1) It's crowned by West Africa's highest peak, Mount Cameroon (Mount Fako to the locals); 2) The isolated Kilim-Ijim ridge in the north-west is the last refuge of the nearly extinct Bannerman's Turaco bird. And 3) Cameroon was recently voted the world's most corrupt nation. The Turaco and Mount Cameroon I was eager to see.

Stepping off the plane it was clear that the place had seen better days. The apparently modern airport walkways had rusted to unusability in the tropical heat. Passengers had to disembark onto the tarmac and trudge for hundreds of sweaty metres through non-airconditioned concrete tubes. At least it wasn't Nigeria, I comforted myself, as I stood dripping with perspiration waiting to have my passport stamped. I had heard dozens of 'Lagos stories' in which arriving passengers had been harassed or ripped off by immigration officials.

So I was pleased to fly on to what I assumed would be the much friendlier Douala — Cameroon's main port city. It was only later that I started hearing very similar stories about Douala.

My mood in the steaming hot atmosphere was hardly improved by talking to fellow travellers. Most had been here before and all but one had either been robbed, or knew someone who had. "That's alright," I said, trying to find a more positive note. It was Mount Cameroon I wanted to see and I'd heard it was a spectacular volcano and a relatively easy climb.

"Climb the mountain? Now? No chance," smirked a perspiration-soaked oil prospector. "It's erupting. Oh, and by the way, whatever you do, don't venture out in Douala at night."

Thus my normally meditative approach to arrival in a new country had been shot to pieces by the time my onward air tickets, visa, and yellow fever certificate had been suitably examined. Tentatively peeping outside the terminal I was immediately caught up in a swirl of grasping arms. Each limb was forcefully directing me to a disorganised selection of taxis, minibuses and beaten up old sedans. Surely most of the drivers were trustworthy. But which? Should I choose from the religious, moral or plain bizarre slogans adorning each vehicle? *Sing Praises* or *The evil that men do, Glory be to God* or *No free lunch, Dig and see* or *Be you green until dust*. One advised simply *Be careful*. The dim illumination cast menacing shadows and the dark faces of the beckoning drivers were impossible to read.

A firm but friendly tap on my shoulder, stronger than the other jostling, disturbed my quandary and I succumbed to the invitation of a relatively genteel chap called Blaise. English-speaking and dapper in a decent suit, he looked a cut above the average. Or did it mean that he was simply better at ripping off the unwary? I was ushered aboard a minibus and suddenly Blaise disappeared. Quietly, two hollow-eyed men in filthy T-shirts, with sizeable knives dangling conspicuously at their sides, appeared out of the shadows.

"Allo *monsieur*," said one of them menacingly, "*S'il vous plaît*," said the other holding out his hand, apparently expecting money. Speaking deliberately poor French I pretended that I thought they were merely greeting me. They closed in. "*Quelque chose monsieur*, something for me." Shadowy hands appeared to fondle the scabbards of their knives.

"We're looking after you, monsieur," said the other darkly. Their faces were growing uncomfortably close, their breath adding a musky odour to the heavy atmosphere in the sweltering van. Then without warning there was a great commotion and clattering of running feet. It was Blaise. Seeing my predicament he and a fellow driver charged at my 'protectors' and sent them fleeing. "Not very good people," he said. It was an understatement.

Blaise himself proved trustworthy. He dropped me safely within the fortified perimeter fence of the hotel I'd chosen, albeit for a very healthy fee. The hotel was an oasis of calm, but the receptionist didn't dampen my sense of paranoia — she too had been mugged by a taxi driver in a secluded underpass. I believed her, and the story encouraged me to hire her brother Ambrose to drive me to Limbe the next morning.

Founded as a German colonial town before the Brits grabbed it as part of First World War reparations, Limbe is a calm, picturesque little seaside town famed for its delightful botanical gardens. Several old wooden hotels maintain a faded grandeur with bow-tied waiters serving cocktails as the sun sets into the silhouette of Malobo Island.

I was silently celebrating having 'survived' Douala, when Ambrose's rickety old Toyota slammed to a halt on the city outskirts. Brusquely awoken from my reverie, I instinctively checked that my money belt was hidden and tensed myself for conflict. The problem proved less severe than I'd feared. It was simply the first of many police road blocks. "You give them 1000CFA (£1) and you go quickly. Don't pay, and you lose your licence. Things get much better when you cross into the anglophone provinces," explained Ambrose.

On the way to Limbe I'd told Ambrose that I lived in Belgium. His reaction was extraordinary, incomprehensible delight. As I was soon to discover, Belgium is famous in Central Africa for only one thing: not chips, not chocolate, but cheap second-hand cars. Within seconds Ambrose was gabbling business ideas. I should buy him a US$1000 Toyota Corolla, nothing fancy of course, but with a start-first-time engine. He'd sell it for $2,000 in a jiffy. I just had to ship it over and he'd pop the money into Western Union for me when the motor had sold. Bob's you're uncle. We'd share the profits. I interrupted and told Ambrose that the shipping would cost a fortune, not to mention the paperwork and the customs.

"That's why we need a Belgian," he gasped as though it was quite obvious. "Antwerp-Douala, you can ship for $700 or $800. See — that's $100 each we make."

That didn't seem a lot of profit to encourage a totally unsecured $1,800 investment. Ambrose detected my inexplicable reticence. "Don't you trust me?" Bizarrely I did. But that wasn't the point. What if anything went wrong? We'd seen how bad the cops were. Unfortunately by this time I'd

25

already given the man my home address and I still get regular mail asking me "Where are the cars?"

Contrary to what my guidebook said, the Bay Hotel in Limbe was certainly not the best choice in town. The motley collection of Nigerian and local guests sat on the peeling wooden terrace, glued to the single fuzzy TV set. In between all-important horse racing and betting reports, the news gave alternating English and French commentaries on the progress of the Mount Cameroon lava flow. It had wiped out houses, ravaged palm groves and had now entirely cut the coastal highway, seven kilometres west of Limbe.

Although all approach roads were now officially barred, crowds of visitors were pictured at the scene. If they could get there, why couldn't I? I decided to give it a try, hitching a ride with a Libyan pipeline consultant and his chuckling chauffeur who were similarly curious. At the inevitable roadblock, police were turning back the light traffic. It was going to take more than 1000CFA to get past the cops here — 5000CFA, to be exact. Plus a story that we had to get to a beach resort which just happened to be the far side of the extraordinary steaming mass of pyroclastic flow. Insanely, souvenir hunters were actually walking on the cooler extremities of the flow where days before the contorted blackened forms had been flaring molten orange. Lava is lava, though. A few minutes was plenty of time to be awed. There was no way I'd be climbing that volcano.

While the French government's policy was to turn its colonial subjects into African Frenchmen, the Brits were happy to leave traditional tribal structures untouched so long as the colony turned a profit. This, combined with poor infrastructure, means that western Cameroonians (known collectively as *Tikaris*), have held onto many of their more colourful ancient tribal traditions, especially in the mountains.

Within Cameroon's North West province alone there are more than 200 monarchs, most known as *Fons*. They rule over an extraordinarily complex patchwork of traditional kingdoms. Some fondoms are mere villages, others like Nso and Bafut, stretch across great swathes of land. These 'first class chiefs' are veritable kings with their own palaces and social hierarchy of lords, *manjong* warrior guards, and harems of wives. I'd never met a king before, and was excited at the prospect of an audience with the Fon of Kom or Oku. But I'd have to wait a few days for an introduction.

Kom is a collection of villages totalling some 140,00' over a considerable area. In contrast, Oku has one mod which sits on a picture-book hillside, shadowed by the ͟ which culminates in the venerable Mount Kilum. The village is ba͟ long rain-eroded laterite road that kinks at the lower end to skirt the sprawling, thatch-roofed palace complex. The road is lined by unremarkable concrete box shops, and thatched shack barber shops with mottos off-beat enough to challenge the Douala taxis: *envy never pays, note this, see fast but don't say fast* and most scarily for a hairdresser: *cut you for God my brother.* The most common business in town is the 'off licence'. An off licence is most definitely not a bar, I was assured by several Guinness-guzzling locals. But the bar stools, glasses and plentiful supply of beer for a crowd of regulars suggested otherwise. Perhaps the defining factor is the volume of the Zingé music that a den can blare.

Behind the hangovers, there are many enlightened projects in Oku — a little handicrafts centre, albeit with no tourists to sell to, a paper co-operative turning out beautiful hand-made greetings cards, and workshops making candles, wax and mead from by-products of the delicious forest honey. There's even a community radio station. Yet behind its modern façade Oku's heart beats to a much more traditional beat, as I saw a few days later when the spirit of death came to town.

Actually there were several spirits in the village that day. An old man from one of the outlying compounds had died and the steep trails between the banana groves and calliandra trees were full of colourfully dressed mourners coming to pay respects. Mourning doesn't describe the atmosphere at all, though. In one darkened hut a huddle of elders made solemn toasts, polishing off an amphora of palm wine in cow horn mugs. But outside there was a buzz of excitement and fun in the air. The majority of the crowd had gathered to see death and chase it away. Death in the form of a *juju.* To the casual outsider, jujus are simply men wearing silly masks and fancy body paint. But within traditional Oku culture they represent all elements of existence. Death in the form of the war juju Labé must be repeatedly banished, Mabu the vandal (a stone-throwing demon who thankfully only appears late at night) must be avoided at all costs, while Nontang the thief has a little harmless fun with unwary visitors. That included me. Beckoning, Nontang seemed to be asking me for my umbrella. My reflex was to hand it over. After a little display of Nontang's

:asure, the trophy was handed to the juju's companions, and off he went.

"But isn't he going to give it back?" I asked a fellow observer.

"What do you think? He's the thief after all."

I'd lost my brolly and my chance to climb Mount Cameroon. But I had unwittingly chosen the perfect time of year for spotting the rare Bannerman's Turaco. The handful of such birds that still survive is attracted to relatively open clearings in the Kilum-Ijim forest by the fruiting of the mossy Nchuin trees. The piously named guide called Godlove was prepared to help me find them.

We tramped gently along glorious woodland paths set with traditional hollowed-log beehives and little noose traps used to collect the popular local snack known as 'Oku Sardines' — roast rat on a stick. The canopy was alive with birdsong: the insistent *chac chak chac chak* of grey apalis and the burbles of chop sisikulas. The *Cha-ka-cha-ka-cha-ka-chaka* cries of Bangwa forest warblers overwhelmed the distant drumming from Nboh village in the valley below.

Then in the distance came the distinctive echoing yelps of two amorous Bannerman's Turacos. Godlove listened intently. Working out the probable direction of the elusive birds, he made an educated guess. We crept through lush glades. Then suddenly Godlove grabbed me. "There," he hissed. And there it was. Patriotically red, gold and green like the national flag, the turaco sat flicking his long noble blue tail and nodding his ruddy crown. Normally intensely shy, it was so preoccupied stuffing fruity morsels into its peanut-shaped beak that it didn't seem to notice the audience. When it finally clattered off into the foliage, Godlove burst with excitement. Bouncing into the air with joy, he admitted it was only the second time in seven years he'd actually seen a Bannerman's Turaco.

Swollen with pride at having seen the rare bird, we retreated from the forest, catching the merest glimpse of a banded wattle eye as we looped back from Kilum lake. Unique to this mountain, the banded wattle eye has been hunted close to extinction for its distinctive red feathers. Worn in a traditional *fundam* hat, the plume denotes that the wearer is a member of the high *kwifon* council and privy to the secrets of the land.

One of the biggest problems in protecting the unique forest is the tension between three distinct tribal groups. Each speaks its own distinctive language, has its own king (fon or ardo) and its own pantheon of juju spirits. The Oku and the Kom are both descended from the same mythical divinities, but over the centuries have become intense rivals occupying opposite sides of the Ijim ridge. The summit itself is occupied by once nomadic Fulani cow herders. The main conflict between all three is based upon neither culture nor religion, but goats. Since tree cutting was banned on Ijim ridge in the mid 1980s, the goats have presented the biggest threat to the forest by chewing bark off the trees and preventing regrowth by nibbling all the saplings. Each ethnic group blames the others for the devilish behaviour of their goats and they occasionally come to blows. When I heard about a 'goat conflict' it sounded trivial and Monty Pythonesque, but as I was soon to discover, it is deadly serious.

The hike into Kom took eight hours up and over the ridge. My Kom guide, Frederic, valiantly carried much of my excessive baggage. On arrival we made the natural decision to soothe our weary limbs with a warm but welcome Mützig lager. "When there's beer, how can I be tired?" beamed Frederic sagely. But his wisdom was interrupted by a great commotion. A band of angry men blustered into the village gesticulating vividly and yelling in cacophonous Kom. Frederic listened aghast. Within seconds he had forgotten his aches and ale. After a few barked conversations with the driver of the Land Rover he jumped aboard and sped off. "Two men hurt," he shouted over his shoulder. "The bastards nearly killed them."

In Kom it had been the traditional day of the royal duck hunt. Since the local duck population has long since been decimated, this is never more than a formality. That year as a confidence-building exercise the palace princes had come up with a novel alternative: head into the forest and hunt illegally grazing goats instead.

This would be politically explosive if attempted without the agreement of their Oku counterparts, but the Oku council (the Kwifon) decided they'd join in. However, the Kom hunting party waited in vain at a neutral clearing for the Oku folk to arrive. When they didn't show, the hunt was called off. Sadly two Kom hunters coming from a distant village arrived too late to hear the news. They had cornered, and were merrily anticipating butchering, a captured goat when spotted from above by the animal's Oku owners. The hunters were ambushed and stoned.

Within the hour the Kom off licences were full of the news. Guinness-fuelled emotions soon had the villagers baying for Oku blood. Tata, an Oku worker at the project with whom I was sharing the primitive guesthouse, was scared witless and refused to go out.

"You'll never get back across to Oku now," he moped.

"Is it that serious?"

"Who knows? I think it might be."

The most radical of the Kom were now calling for a war against Oku.

"We're three times stronger than they are, we'd beat them any day. It's time someone taught those Oku a leson," said Ivo, a previously mild-mannered medic.

"You wouldn't really go to war, would you?" I asked. "Tribal wars don't really happen these days do they?"

"Not often," was his unreassuring response. "The last time we fought Oku was only a little war."

"What does little mean?"

"Well, one village was burnt but only 30 or so died. Anyway that was years and years ago."

"Like, 19th century?"

"Oh, no, 1986 I think."

Everything hinged on the Fon. He would have to make a formal decision. My audience at the palace was also to be the next morning. Innocent, my guide, now had two tasks of very unequal importance. 1) Introduce me. 2) Avert war at all costs.

The King of Kom's palace is at Liakom, a royal village high up an isolated, unsurfaced red scar of laterite track beneath the ominously named 'executioner's ridge'. The scenery is an abstract collection of bald, steeply grassy hills in eccentric knobs and sugar loaves. The main patch of woodland, an extremely lush copse known as Lumutu, was the 'secret medicine forest', where only princes and the Fon's witch doctors are allowed to harvest leaves, bark and mysterious berries for use in special potions.

The palace itself nestles in a small amphitheatre on the edge of the medicine forest. The exterior fences are draped in beautiful solanium vines whose trumpet-shaped lily flowers hang heavily like bells. The shrub's wide leaves were formerly used as serving platters for royal banquets. These days their status has fallen distinctly. With the advent of plastic plates, alternative uses have been found for the leaves and now they are known in the Kom language as *Ufue-aghal* (toilet-wipes).

Behind the floral drapes, the palace is clearly very old. Rock platforms and intriguing carved stones are covered in lichen and moss. But the whole ensemble could not be described as visually beautiful. Old harem houses and royal structures are patched up with too much unaesthetic rusty corrugated metal roofing and unadorned concrete filler. Still, the approach to the royal court is quite a labyrinth and knowing that 'forbidden zones' are protected by jujus, guards and magic spells, I was suitably awed. We emerged into the central courtyard through a flapping metal curtain.

Wow. I had walked straight into *Alice in Wonderland*. The mad hatter's tea party appeared to be in full swing. It was difficult to believe. The land was on the verge of war — were these reeling old fellows really about to decide the fate of thousands?!

The enclosure was rectangular, stepped with ancient hewn stones on three sides and open to the air. In the centre sat the Fon. His throne was modest and covered by a maharaja-style canopy. Around him, each in a position designated by age, family and social status, sat a motley selection of colourfully dressed princes, elders and followers. Some swayed gently, almost dozing off to sleep until shaken awake to answer very occasional royal mutterings. Several appeared drunk. But the most startling feature of the court was that absolutely nothing happened... for minutes at a time. Everyone seemed to be waiting for something.

Having sat patiently outside for several minutes, our entry into the arena didn't cause the slightest visible reaction. Finally a palace helper scurried delicately across and ushered us forward, placing us almost in front of the Fon. Like Victorian children, no visitor, except the highest ranked prince, would dare to speak until spoken to in the regal presence. And the Fon didn't look talkative. So we stood there in the middle of the court for several anxious minutes, heads bowed modestly, awaiting permission to introduce ourselves. He said nothing. We said nothing. He lit a cigarette and gazed into space. Dressed in T-shirt and track suit, puffing idly on a Marlboro, he didn't exactly fit my image of an African king.

Finally, after humbling us suitably with the long silence, the Fon turned to Innocent and asked him to introduce us. "*Mbe*," said Innocent, with bowed head and fist clenched lightly across his mouth, as etiquette demands. After an indecipherable string of obsequiousness and greetings our presentation of gifts could proceed. One advantage of visiting a Fon is that there's never any doubt about what to buy him — whisky.

31

"Now," whispered Innocent. With a bow towards the throne I passed the locally purchased bottle of J&B Rare (marked '*For sale in Cameroon only*' and costing a mere £2.50). It was passed to one of the serving courtiers who placed it with the dozen or so similar bottles that had been delivered by earlier arrivals.

"He'll be wasted if he drinks all of that," I whispered to Innocent later once we'd been ushered to our places.

"He won't," said Innocent. "But you might have to."

I laughed. "Seriously?"

Shortly afterwards the chief palace steward collected up some of the bottles and started distributing them amongst the assorted 'guests'. I soon understood why so many of them swayed — each bottle delivered had to be finished by the recipient before he (and they were all 'hes') could decently expect to leave. Drinking from ceremonial cow horns, each guest was quickly supping away with exaggerated glee, if surreptitiously taking care to spill a fair percentage on the weathered rock seats. Whether by luck or through compassion on the only weak-livered white-man, we 'only' received a single token bottle between us. Still plenty, however, to relax a little and to start to blur one's memory of the arcane palace rules. And the rules are very easy to break. Crossing your legs, drinking with the left hand, failing to bow when crossing the Fon's line of sight — all are crimes punishable with a fine denominated in goats.

In the meantime one of the most bellicose of the high princes had finally found his feet and was making a forceful if rambling speech about the Oku situation. His view was clear — now was the time to launch an attack. The mood of his colleagues seemed to be leaning towards war. Innocent, wearing a new metaphorical cap altogether, was invited to give a counter-argument. After his calm speech the Fon retired to consider.

Horns filled with more whisky. And everybody waited. And waited.

Finally after an interminable pause, the courtiers returned and started to dress up the throne with oddments of carpet and tie-dye. Cowry-covered pots were placed on either side, and an elephant's tusk and jaguar skin were laid for the royal footrest. The Fon re-emerged magnificently re-dressed in full scarlet and blue regalia.

We held our breath as he spoke.

After the pomp of his re-entry, his words were short and to the point.

"Stop all this talk of war. Go and hunt me some ducks."

A Tanzanian ferry tale

by Anna Rockall

A blond moustachioed Stanley stands, hat in hand and mouth forever frozen open in greeting to a dark moustachioed Livingstone. Livingstone's mouth is closed — history does not relate his reply to Stanley's famously understated "Dr Livingstone, I presume." That this example of colonial composure should even be remembered is surprising enough; that the spot where it was said should be marked with a plaque, a papier-mâché statue and what passes for a museum is little short of absurd.

But if it's absurdity you want, then this memorial in Ujiji had it by the bucketload, all under the shade of a mango tree grafted from the original that Livingstone was sitting under when Stanley arrived. The guide sat me down and launched into a mesmerising recitation of the life of Livingstone, a speech he had clearly made so many times that he didn't have to think about the words. He took a deep breath, and the words fell out of his mouth at a higher and higher pitch, until the sound of his voice had turned from the grumble of a waiting car to the whine of a moped going up a hill. He had an accent, but more noticeable was his habit of adding 'y' and 'mmm' to the ends of words: "When Livingstone diedymmm, they took out his hearty and intestinesmmm, and preserved him in spicey and salt to be buried in Europemmmm." It was difficult to follow the bizarre undulations of the guide's voice. It didn't matter.

Ujiji is on the shores of Lake Tanganyika, in the west of Tanzania. Not many of the tourists who crowd the Serengeti and Zanzibar make it to this side of the country, so locals make their living without the help of the lucrative tourist dollar. Ujiji's beach is not for sunbathing, but for fishing, washing and mending nets and building boats. It was an industrious stretch — several *dhows* and *mokoros* pulled up on the shore were surrounded by the debris of crabs and fish bones which crunched underfoot. Evil-smelling fish lay in a basket ready to be sold. Two old men sat in the shade sorting through the nets; another was weaving reed traps. One man hammered at a small boat, a few more were working on a large dhow, a couple of women were washing clothes, and naked children played in the shallows. The lake is their life.

Across the water lies the Democratic Republic of Congo. Usually hidden by the haze, it was lit up that evening by a sunset that seemed to set fire to the mountains and turn the water red. To the north is Rwanda and Burundi. This corner of Tanzania is peaceful enough, but it has troubled neighbours; the luxury 4WDs of aid workers from the nearby refugee camps are often seen on the streets of Kigoma, the region's main town. Four-wheel drives around here are useful things — Kigoma is an off-road kind of town, with only two sealed streets and more potholes than people. There's not a lot to the place — it has a few shops, a market, and the crumbled magnificence of the railway station with its glorious arched windows and dirty peeling paint.

Despite the fact there is nothing much there, it's an important junction — the railway leads to Dar es Salaam, and the ferry travels 500km down Lake Tanganyika to Zambia. Lake Tanganyika is the second deepest lake in the world, and part of the Great Rift Valley, where millions of years ago tectonic plates tore against each other in a gargantuan attempt to rip Africa in half. The ferry *MV Mwongozo* plies its waters every week, delivering goods and trading opportunities to the isolated villages along the Tanzanian shoreline. For most of the villagers this is their only contact with the outside world.

A couple of hundred people boarded the ferry in Kigoma, scrambling over the ranks of oil drums which were being loaded by the same entrance. We left port only two hours late, which by local standards is pretty good. Tanzanians are not slaves to the clock, and although the ferry schedule might say it leaves at 3pm on Wednesday and arrives at 8am on Friday, this is really just a guideline. It leaves when it's ready, and it arrives when it gets there. Asking how long a journey will take is a hard habit to break, but any answer you get is invariably useless.

My second class bunk would have been hot, smelly and cramped in any circumstances, but it was made worse by the fact the four-berth cabin was sleeping six that night, plus some sacks of maize. The bunks were cunningly made of plastic to encourage the maximum amount of sweating and the window looked out onto a dank corridor where water from leaking pipes sloshed on the floor. The only thing I could be glad about was that I wasn't in third class — a dark and cluttered room full of people sprawling uncomfortably on wooden benches, slumped on the floor, and crammed together in the stifling heat. In many respects my bunk was little better, but at least I had space to lie down.

The upper deck was a much more congenial place than my cabin in which to spend time as we sailed past mountains and beaches. My fellow passengers, knowing we were all going to be together for two days, were friendly, despite my lack of Swahili. Children, though, don't need words — they need paper boats, clapping games, and face-pulling competitions. It was all very sweet — until they started to multiply. Suddenly I was surrounded by 30 children, all shouting at me in Swahili and wanting attention. My paper boat-making skills went to pot under the pressure, and I was forced to resign my position as chief children's entertainer.

When night fell, the glow of storm lanterns on the fishing boats danced across the lake, strung out like fairy lights along the horizon. A huge Congolese businesswoman in a bright pink shirt chatted to me in French about fishing, war and her husband. I was beginning to relax. I no longer felt alone in a sea of strangers. There were also the other travellers, a Canadian couple and a Dutch couple, and after the obligatory conversation about the state of our bowels we were all on friendly terms.

Dinner in the restaurant was a surprisingly civilised affair, considering how many people they were trying to feed, but it was a simple enough menu — beef rice or chicken rice. Just as I finished my meal, the ship's horn sounded and we slid gently to a halt. Clambering up to the deck I could see our searchlights scanning the shore, and despite the fact it that looked as uninhabited as any other bit we'd passed, it was clear we were about to get mobbed.

About 15 boats — dugout canoes, rowing boats, a few motor boats and a couple of big dhows carrying 30 or so people each — were speeding towards us as fast as they could. The motor boats had the obvious advantage, and were leading the way. Then came the canoeists and the rowers, straining every muscle to get to the ferry first. The heavier boats were slower, but probably felt less urgency as they had already earnt a few thousand shillings that evening from passenger fares. The rest were relying on trade with the ferry, and everything depended on a good position next to the doorway.

The smaller boats were selling snacks of fish and *ugali* wrapped in a banana leaf, roasted corn on the cob, or grilled fish. Those on the lower decks could reach the sellers, but passengers on the upper decks had to catch the food which was tossed up to them, and drop the money down. The air was thick with flying corn and sardines. The middling boats were picking up parcels of household goods and soft drinks to deliver to the village, where they would get paid a small amount for transporting them. The more parcels they picked up, the more they would earn that night. Competition was fierce, consideration and support for fellow villagers non-existent. The opportunity to trade arose for ten minutes, twice a week, and it was a dog-eat-dog affair.

They shouted, swore and pushed each other's boats out of the way. One man started stealing parcels from a neighbouring boat until he was punched in the face by the wronged boatman. Another furiously snatched a Muslim's hat from his head and threw it into the lake for the same reason. Somebody slipped and went overboard, and when he tried to scramble into the nearest boat — not his own — he was repeatedly bashed over the head with a plastic water scoop until he gave up and dropped back into the lake. Considering the amount of water they were taking on board it was a miracle nobody sank, but in between tussles they would quickly bale out the bottom of the boat before getting back to business. One woman, baling out at the same time as shouting at someone, never noticed the scoop she was using had an enormous hole in it.

After another huge honk from the ferry, the doors were shut and we moved on, leaving the villagers to settle their differences until the next time. There were regular stops like this throughout the journey, and on each occasion the arrival of the ferry served as a starter's gun for a ferocious race. One middle-of-the-night stop took rather longer than the rest. After the dhows dropped off their passengers, the merchants started to unload bales and bales of goods which were hoisted onto the front of the ferry by a crane. Three hundred bales, it turned out to be, and what was in them became clear as the smell crept over the decks — dried sardines that had been sitting in the sun for a week. From then on it was scarcely necessary to sound the horn to announce our arrival, as we wafted down the lake in a cloud of fish fumes.

A sweaty night in the cabin was made worse, not only by the stench of fish, which had permeated through the boat, but also by the fact I had to remain clothed because anyone could see through the window. I dreamt enviously of the first class cabins, which were quiet, clean and reasonably spacious (though still hot and stinking of sardines). I eventually drifted off to sleep, waking just before dawn. There were showers on board, but there was no way I was going to use them as that would have meant staying in the vicinity of the toilets longer than I could hold my breath. I won't dwell too much on the sanitary arrangements, except to say that I deliberately became dehydrated during the journey so I could keep my number of trips to the ladies to a bare minimum.

I watched the pink sun rise over the mists of the Mahale Mountains National Park as I brushed my teeth over the side of the boat. The sleeping bodies that littered the decks stirred and shivered in the dawn wind as the boat gradually came to life. That second day was to be spent entirely on the boat, and there was a relaxed atmosphere as we idly watched the silver-blue water and hot-yellow beaches slipping by, and the shore flattening out as we drifted further south. It was hazy and humid, and the drowsy passengers drifted in and out of sleep. Even the traders seemed less desperate than those the previous night, heaving the goods on and off the boats with a little more decorum than their neighbours.

Despite the evident poverty of the villagers, many of whom wore barely identifiable rags, they were in the kind of physical condition that Westerners put a lot of time, effort and money into achieving. Living by the lake they clearly never had problems finding a water supply, and so they could irrigate crops, water animals, and of course they had a never-ending supply of fish. Life was no doubt hard and without much in the way of luxuries, but hunger and thirst were strangers to them and they seemed to be a picture of health and physical fitness.

That evening we stopped for the first time at a village which was connected by road — or track to be more precise — to the rest of the country, and so for the first time a significant amount of people got off the ferry. Nearly 100 people hustled on board the waiting dhows to be taken to shore. I watched them chug off into the distance, and settled in for my second night on the boat. The feeling onboard inevitably changed once there were fewer people — it was less frenetic, quieter and more spacious. Dinner in the restaurant almost felt as if we were aboard a cruise ship, only without the glitter balls and dancing girls.

Now that there was more room on the boat, I decided to try and find space on deck to sleep rather than descend into the pit below. But getting the necessary space involved tactics I hadn't employed since leaving junior school. A few hours before bedtime, I chose a well-positioned bench out of the wind. I sat squarely in the middle, and started the slow process of spreading; when the woman on my right wandered off, my belongings inched over until they had taken over that side, while I kept the spatial pressure up on my left until I was clearly the dominating presence on the bench. Then in a proprietorial kind of way, I swung my feet up and claimed my sleeping area. All over the deck similar manoeuvrings were taking place, and once established, you couldn't move as you would immediately be replaced my someone else. It was hardly worth it for comfort's sake, as the narrow benches required absolute immobility, but the cooling breeze and freely circulating air made the upper deck the most pleasant place on the ferry. Apart from the brief interruption of a fist fight in the small hours, it was a comparatively comfortable night.

At 5am we pulled into the first proper dock of the journey, at the village of Kasanga. This was the last stop before the terminus in Zambia, and time for me to bail out, so to speak.

I had been assured I could find transport at Kasanga, and sure enough a big open-backed truck sat waiting for passengers and goods from the ferry. I hopped on board and sat on top of a sack of grain, and waited in the pre-dawn darkness for more food to be loaded. When 20 passengers had managed to squeeze on we trundled slowly down the track through the fields of maize and open pastures.

It soon became clear that this was not going to be an easy journey. The truck stopped at each little village to unload a few things and pick up a lot more, so that each stop raised the difficult question of how to cram more goods on board. At one point I counted 24 adults, three babies, 15 planks of wood, an estimated 40 sacks of grain, piles and piles of personal baggage and, of course, a chicken. Most of us were sitting scrunched up, knees pulled to chin, leaning against each other for balance on the bumpy road. We maintained this position for seven hours.

We were all getting cosy after five hours on the road when the darkening sky rumbled, roared and spat at us. I had forgotten that by travelling south in February I was going to run into the rainy season, so there I was, open to the elements on the back of a truck wearing only shorts and T-shirt. My fellow travellers pulled out what they had in the way of wet weather gear —which in many cases was not much — but my pack was buried out of reach. I resigned myself to a soggy journey.

Fortunately, others were more enterprising than me, and a tarpaulin was located — awkwardly buried under several hundred kilograms of goods. A struggle to free it ensued, involving a lot of shouting, someone getting accidentally pushed off the truck (which had at least stopped), and tempers, including mine, flaring freely. We wriggled, yanked and tore the tarpaulin free, and then held it over our heads while the truck ground through the muddy track.

I couldn't see the road ahead, but looking back I was often surprised that we had managed to plough through the great mire of water without stalling, or cross potholes so huge that we surely should have tipped on to our side. Eventually it happened — we became stuck in the mud, our wheels spinning fruitlessly no matter how loudly the engine revved. At least it had stopped raining, though that didn't make much difference with the wheels whipping up plenty of water from below. Out we all jumped. For once there was an advantage in all the overcrowding and we easily, if muddily, pushed the vehicle out of trouble.

Apart from one brief stop for sweet milky *chai* and deep-fried 'half-cakes' in a little village, we didn't get another chance to stretch our legs until we shuddered into Sumbawanga after seven hours on the road. I was expecting to spend the night there before catching the onward bus at 6am, but for once I got lucky. A bus had broken down an hour out of town, and the hapless passengers had been waiting all day for the guilty part to be fixed.

It meant that I had no time to explore Sumbawanga, but a five-minute walk around the muddy streets assured me that although it was a strangely appealing little place, I was not missing much. Just as we arrived, a jeep was preparing to deliver the necessary bits to the distressed bus and get it on its way again. I jumped in and joined up with the other passengers, with only a short wait while they changed the part.

Everyone was taking it very stoically. They were all lying in the long grass on the verge, chatting and relaxing. Someone had started a fire and was roasting corn cobs, so I bought one for five pence and sat down to wait. Considerately, the sun shone until the moment we boarded, then it started to bucket down. But luck was travelling with me. The bus was falling to bits and the seats were as comfortable as an iron trapeze, but we only had one puncture, which took a mere half hour to fix, and I rocked into Mbeya at 11pm, exhausted but triumphant. It had been one hell of a day.

Mbeya is the first main Tanzanian stop for the international train from Lusaka in Zambia to Dar es Salaam. It's a big town, and I wandered around the busy streets looking for something to admire. I soon realised there wasn't much to see. It is too developed to be unusual, but not wealthy enough for interesting architecture. Instead, I stopped for beef samosas — a ubiquitous snack which I had been convinced would make me gut-wrenchingly ill the first time I tried it, but which had resolutely failed to do so — and chai. It was the local equivalent of crisps and a coke.

Later that afternoon, and armed with a first-class ticket (I'd had enough of tough travelling) I boarded, feeling excited at moving on to the last leg of my journey. The four-bunk compartment was comfortable with plenty of space — or at least it was until the women I was sharing it with started to ship in their cargo of a couple of great sacks of potatoes and grain, boxes and suitcases by the dozen. Soon our luxurious compartment was familiarly cramped and uncomfortable. Luckily there were only three of us, so the extra bed carried most of the excess, and international relations in the room were maintained.

An hour out of Mbeya we ground to a halt. There was no village to be seen, let alone a station, but along the tracks 50 or so people made the most of an opportunity to sell their produce to passing clientele. Potatoes and carrots seemed to be the main commodity, and a roaring trade was done as passengers leant out of the windows and started buying in bulk. This was clearly a cheap place to buy, as both of my companions invested in big bags of carrots, and the traders were happy to be selling so much without having to transport it to a market.

The children in the tiny thatch and mud-brick villages we passed did well, too. The train slowed as we went past lines of kids along the track, who stood waving and calling to the passengers. I asked my companions for a translation; they wanted our empty water bottles so they could carry drinking water on the long hot walk to school. It was a reasonable enough request, and all along the train plastic bottles flew out of the windows, the children laughing as they raced along the track to pick them up.

The women in my compartment passed the time knitting doilies, one in the most hideous fluorescent orange wool. As we rolled by the waterlogged rice fields they tried in vain to teach me a few words of Swahili and chatted about my marriage prospects. "You're not married? At 27? Why? What's wrong with you?" In an attempt to escape the increasingly personal conversation I walked down the train to third class to visit some fellow travellers I'd met at the station. I was expecting it to be dark, stinking and overcrowded like the ferry, so was a little taken aback to find a perfectly comfortable carriage which only had the disadvantage of having nowhere to stretch out at night. It would be a rough sleep for the Australian couple I left there, but otherwise it wasn't bad.

I admit that I slept luxuriously, lulled by the jolting train which only once jolted hard enough to crack my head against the side table.

At dawn the train entered the Selous Game Reserve. I won't see much, I thought, maybe a few antelope. But as the sun rose the first thing I saw was a herd of wildebeest swishing their tails in a grove of thick-trunked baobab trees. I curled up by the window and watched a herd of zebra kicking their heels up at the passing train, a giraffe startled into a loping canter, impala nibbling at the damp morning grass, and a warthog trotting idly by. Even at our speed, I saw the bright flash of a lilac-breasted roller, and a group of saddle-billed storks wading in a pool of white waterlilies. And most surprisingly, I saw a leopard stretching and preening itself by the side of the track, clearly unfussed by the thunder of the train. Considering we were charging through at 80kph and making enough noise to wake the dead, it was a pretty successful safari.

My journey had looped southern Tanzania, keeping me well away from the tourist crowds of Ngorongoro, Serengeti, Zanzibar and Kilimanjaro, and as the train brought me ever closer to Dar es Salaam, I realised that getting 'off the beaten track', that traveller's holy grail, had only taken a little extra effort and imagination. OK, I hadn't blazed any trails, but I'd travelled through parts of the country only a few travellers reached, and seen the side of Tanzania that survived on subsistence farming rather than tourist dollars. I sat in the train restaurant waiting for breakfast, feeling that somehow it might have been more intrepid to go in third class. I couldn't deny, though, that seeing this bit from the comfort of a dining car made it all the more enjoyable.

Southern Africa's empty quarter

by Matt Rudd

I know Victoria Falls is in Africa, but after three days there it just didn't feel like Africa. Yes, I'd seen hippos and elephants above the waterfall and crocodiles beneath it. And I'd been served a beer at the very traditional Victoria Falls hotel by a man in a starchy uniform with brass buttons. I'd seen some disproportionately large sunsets and I'd even been bitten by mosquitoes which, though hardly a positive experience, is nonetheless an African one.

But I still felt more like I was in an American theme park than at the heart of southern Africa. The hippos and elephants were spotted from a boat packed with almost as much alcohol as tourists. The raft on which I'd paddled past the crocodiles was captained by a surfer from California. And I'd been staying in a campsite inhabited by bungee jumpers, frisbee throwers and fire jugglers. I wouldn't deny that I was enjoying myself, but considering this was only the second stop on my supposed African adventure, I was beginning to get nervous that there wasn't going to be much adventure at all.

So you can imagine my relief two days later as I sat by the side of a dusty road examining a blown tyre in the company of at least 20 motionless San bushmen. Victoria Falls, with its burger bars and scenic air tours, was 300km and two countries back the way we'd come, and Angola, always a slightly intimidating country to be near, was a few kilometres to the north. Brought up on politically incorrect Tarzan films and made paranoid by gloomy Foreign Office advice, I was feeling particularly nervous about how the situation might unfold.

Not surprisingly, my fears were unfounded. A Coke offering to the head of the San broke the ice, and by the time the tyre had been replaced, we were all dancing to the tunes of a tinny portable radio. Us Westerners were attempting to teach the waltz. The bushmen were demonstrating a more co-ordinated tribal dance. Not a good exercise in anthropology, but at least here, halfway along a spindly finger of Namibia, I was beginning to feel as though I was in Africa.

The Caprivi Strip is a fantastic example of what happens when you let two 19th century colonial powers sit down at a conference table in Europe with maps, red pens and a few bottles of claret. Count von Caprivi, the enthusiastic German chancellor at the time, wanted to link his new bit of empire, south-west Africa, with trade routes in the east. Unhelpfully, but rather typically, Britain had assumed control of most of the territory in between. So after a long chat in Berlin, Britain let Germany annex a 500km-long corridor of land running all the way to within a few miles of Zimbabwe in return for Zanzibar.

On reflection, a beautiful spice island in return for some remote scrubland might have seemed like a good deal for the Brits, but it was strategy, strategy, strategy in those days. The corridor was named after the chancellor and, after some chop and change during the 20th century, the Caprivi Strip is part of Namibia today.

To drive along this spur of imperial folly had sounded like an exciting idea when we planned the trip from the comfort of a flat in London. We had pictured golden sunsets, steady progress, encounters with wildlife and wholesome camp experiences. The guidebooks even said it was fertile and green. But by the end of a second day of heat, dust and flat, straight roads, the novelty was beginning to wear off. We'd seen nothing but a few giraffe, and my dust bowl preconceptions of south-west Africa were beginning to be fulfilled. Other than that, it was slowly dawning on me that distances in Africa are huge. We'd listened to three decent tapes to the point of irritation, and even Billy Joel — packed accidentally of course — was getting the occasional airtime.

Tyre trouble wasn't helping either, but at least we had a meteorite to look forward to. Day three was Hoba Meteorite day and I sprung from my sleeping bag with all the enthusiasm you'd expect of someone who'd seen nothing for three days. Only a shortish detour from the endless Golden Highway, we were hardly going to pass up the opportunity to see it. As we trundled up a dirt road from Grootfontein, I imagined Hoba, the largest meteorite ever discovered, would be at least half the size of New York, something that would have turned day into night and shaken the earth to its core on impact.

In reality, Hoba is nothing more than a relatively small lump of iron in the ground. It might have killed a couple of unfortunate elephants but, to my intense disappointment, it wasn't the apocalyptic mountain of doom I had been expecting.

And so we headed back to the road, trying hard not to gnaw our legs off with deepening road boredom. Salvation came later that day with our arrival in Etosha. My guidebooks all raved about Etosha, ranking it alongside Kruger and the Serengeti as one of Africa's great game-viewing parks. Even this high accolade didn't prepare me for the teeming multitudes of birds and animals I saw eking out an existence in this desolate landscape.

You always hear how David Attenborough film crews spend months hiding in bushes waiting for the right animals to come along. Here they must get through a couple of reels a day. Most of Noah's key players roam freely and prolifically across the flat plains and, unlike the sad zoo animals I remembered from my childhood, they are completely wild. It's an obvious point, but it startles you when you see it for real.

Having checked in at Namutoni Camp, a fenced-in island of tents and lodges in this sea of raw Etosha wilderness, I walked down to the watering hole. It was getting on for sunset, the traditional happy hour for African wildlife.

Each rank of animal has its own approach to the watering process. First to arrive were the zebra and antelope, tiptoeing out of the darkness to neck a few pints before high-tailing it back into the bush. Their eyes bulged with anxiety and I tried to imagine what it must be like to spend your entire life in fear of being eaten.

Further up the food chain, a gang of rhino arrived, as nonchalant as you like, to share a leisurely drink with an equally blasé herd of buffalo.

And then, just as the sun dipped below the horizon, a raucous family of adolescent elephants barged in by the most direct route possible, taking care not to avoid any obstructing vegetation. The gentlemen's club atmosphere of the rhino was destroyed in an instant as the elephants entertained themselves with their built-in water pistols.

For three nights I slept out in hope of seeing lion. Every few hours, a roar had the whole camp up and running to the waterhole in anticipation. But sound travels well on still African nights, and even though the passing pride sounded like it was just over the brow of the hill, the rangers always told us that they were several kilometres away.

"It's right that a king should have some mystique, mate," explained an Australian who had also decided to sleep out by the waterhole. "Your royals should take a leaf out of his book."

I'm one of those travellers who always misses something by a day. I've been on three whale-watching cruises and never seen a whale. It was always the cruise before mine that had seen every type in existence, usually somersaulting and pirouetting within metres of the boat. The same goes for yellow-eyed penguins in New Zealand. I sat in a freezing hide for six hours with a penguin enthusiast telling me he'd seen them come in every day for the last three weeks and couldn't understand why they'd decided not to bother that day.

So on my fourth and final day in Etosha, I'd already resigned myself to the fact that animals worldwide were determined to avoid me and that I wasn't going to see lion in the wild.

But then it happened. As we trundled along in an open-top truck, a lioness crossed just metres in front of us, followed by six lively young cubs doing their best to annoy her. She had the look of a harassed mother trying to deal with tired children in a shopping centre. Quite understandably, we were the least of her worries and she didn't even glance up. Within seconds, she and her rabble were gone. We continued towards camp and I was delighted.

Of course, lions are like buses — none for ages then ten at once. Around the next corner we interrupted a large male lion trying to have a special moment with his partner. The couple didn't seem too embarrassed by our presence and soon picked up where they'd left off. It was a brief, unimpressive display, and the king of the jungle was starting to lose street cred in front of his audience of safari trucks.

Until, that is, a Japanese tourist stepped down from the truck behind ours to get a closer photograph. The lion was on his feet in seconds, the lioness looking away uninterested as he advanced with powerful, rapid steps towards the tourist. Such a lightning transformation, from inept lover to mighty predator, took us all by surprise, not least the tourist. Faced with the concept of a rapidly approaching lion, he wisely decided against the photo and dived unceremoniously back on board. No one laughed because we had all seen the danger in the situation.

To the south of the sparse plains of the Etosha Pan, the knee-high scrub and leafless thickets give way to the spectacular canyons, valleys and mountains of Damaraland. I had felt isolated enough travelling across the Caprivi Strip, but here we didn't pass a vehicle or village for hours at a time.

Namibia has one of the lowest population densities in the world, but even by Namibian standards Damaraland is especially lacking in people. It would be the ideal place to set up a 'confront-your-fears' clinic for agoraphobics, although some would say that might be bordering on unnecessary cruelty.

By the afternoon we reached Twyfelfontein, said to be the finest neolithic site ever discovered, with more than 2,500 rock paintings dating from 300BC. Unlike Hoba this was well worth the hike, not just for the beautiful etchings, but for the staggering views across the Aba-Huab river. It has a different feel to other parts of Africa. From a rocky outcrop, I could see across valleys for miles in almost every direction. Because humanity had made no impact on anything before me, it felt empty and lifeless, despite its rugged beauty.

That night we camped in the middle of nowhere, passing the evening exchanging travel tales around an insubstantial fire. I'd grown used to orchestras of crickets, but the odd growl or cackle — which I heard coming from the surrounding hills — weren't quite so comforting. According to a ranger we had met the previous day, a man had died in these parts after being dragged from his tent by a crazed hyena.

"He'd forgotten to zip his tent to the very bottom," said the ranger, as though the man had all but asked to be dragged from the tent by his head. This played on my mind, as did a story an old Zimbabwean friend had once told me about his friend Jeanette.

They had decided to camp out in the bush one night at the age of nine or ten. In the middle of the night Jeanette had dreamt she was eating jelly and ice cream. She woke with eight enormous spider legs around her mouth, having already swallowed the head and abdomen. She still suffers from acute arachnophobia today.

I looked up at the moon to relax and we talked for a while about the vivid constellations in the African sky. I looked down again to find a small scorpion climbing determinedly up my boot. I kicked it away in a near-hysterical display of impromptu martial arts.

"Only a small one," I said to make myself feel better.

"Small ones are the worst," said my friend. "They won't kill you but the pain is so bad you'll want to cut your own leg off to make it go away." I slept fitfully, even though I'd checked the zip on my tent ten times.

After the loneliness of Damaraland, it never occured to me that anywhere in Namibia would be booked out. But when we reached Swakapmund, an isolated town on the Namibian coast, we found we were to be the honorary Josephs and Marys of the evening. Every single place in town was full and we were forced to drive to a campsite exposed to the stormy ocean winds. There was one bungalow left. It was sparse, unattractive and the only view was of the main shower block, but after five days of hard travel and water rations, this basic set-up felt like the Hilton. I hadn't been travelling long enough to reject all Western comforts completely.

My Swakapmund guidebook told a story that summed up the delights of the north Namibian coast. More than 500 years ago, a brave Portuguese explorer, Diego Cao, was ordered by his king to round the southern cape of Africa and discover a route to the spice centres of the East. Having got as far as Angola, Cao concluded, reasonably enough, that there was no end to Africa and returned home to break the bad news. But the unsympathetic king sent Cao off again and this time he got as far as the barren and jagged coast of Namibia. Angola had been bad, but Namibia was obviously too much for him. After setting up a cross, he got back on his boat and died a broken man.

I sympathised with Cao as I stood at the cross the following morning nursing a hangover. He wouldn't have had the benefit of a charming town and its many colonial bars to keep the elements at bay. Today

Swakapmund is Namibia's principal holiday resort, but Cao's only escape from the Atlantic would have been the equally inhospitable desert interior.

A day's drive south along winding mountain roads lies an oasis called Sesreim, acting as a base camp to the highest sand dunes in the world. We arrived two hours before sunset and, feeling in need of adventure after the home comforts of Swakapmund, decided to walk five kilometres around a large hill to Sesreim Canyon.

Three others from the campsite joined us for the trek, and within the hour we were happily installed in the beautiful canyon for sundown. It was only as darkness fell, and we started to have trouble picking our way back through the canyon, that we realised no one had thought to bring a torch or water. True, we weren't expedition experts. We couldn't be expected to carry flares or emergency blankets or global positioning systems. But surely a torch wasn't too much to ask? Apparently it was, which we all thought rather amusing until I fell into a ditch and someone else stubbed a toe.

And then, as happens in all good survival movies, discord in the group began. We were standing in front of the hill between us and our campsite and a decision had to be made. I wanted to go over the hill while there were still some vestiges of light. Alan said it looked more like a mountain than a hill and wanted to go around it. Eloise, a usually sensible traveller, was determined to stay put and wait for help. Someone mentioned snakes. Someone else noted the rapidly falling temperature. None of us, it transpired, had been in the scouts.

We argued as though our lives depended on it, mainly because we thought they did. After some swearing and a few this-is-just-typicals and I-told-you-we-shouldn't-haves, a compromise was reached. We would go over the hill/mountain, but I would lead the way in case of any unexpected holes or lethal reptiles. I felt I'd come out of the debate quite badly, but as we began the ascent a miraculous thing happened. The moon popped up above the horizon and we could see our way ahead. By the time we clambered to the top of the hill, the campsite was clearly visible and the sand dunes below us were cast in an eerie white light. The argument was forgotten as we all congratulated ourselves on our fantastic survival skills. We even ran the last few hundred metres out of relief, pretending the white dunes were snow drifts.

To catch the dunes of Sossusvlei at their daybreak best, we had to leave Sesreim at 5am. I was woken before my alarm went off by a fierce wind howling against the walls of my tent. Still half-asleep, I gathered my towel and toothbrush and stepped out into what I soon realised was the heart of a ferocious sandstorm. I turned back in time to see my whole tent blow away with my backpack and clothesline in tow. Speechless, I turned back into the wind to see if anyone else was having similar difficulties and got a mouthful of sand for my troubles. Add the windburn, sand blindness and sub-zero dawn temperatures and you'd probably agree I had a rude, if not unusual awakening to life in the Namibian desert.

But it was worth it. The storm soon passed and as we reached the Sossusvlei dunes we let out a communal gasp of wonderment. Whatever you hear about other parts of the world, I absolutely guarantee that they won't be more beautiful or awesome than Sossusvlei. I stumbled along the last few metres of the track trying to comprehend the enormity of what towered before me.

The bright red dunes, cut smoothly by contoured ridges and shadow, rise up more than 300 metres to touch the deep blue sky. If this had been America, there would have been an ice cream kiosk at the bottom, souvenir stalls at the top and Photo Opportunity areas along the way. Here in this strange and secret place, we were the only evidence of human existence.

I set off with a few embarrassed whoops and hollers and almost instantaneously found that climbing a sand mountain is much harder than it looks. It's a very similar sensation to one of those gym step machines. No matter how fast you step, you still don't feel like you're getting anywhere. My first tactic was to take several big strides as quickly as possible and then rest. Of course I was exhausted after a couple of minutes and ended up adopting a Monty Pythonesque stagger in the style of someone lost for days in the desert.

An hour and several hallucinations later, I was walking along the crescent of the world's highest dune. Far beneath us, another group of impressed travellers was beginning the ascent. In every direction for as far as the eye could see there were swirling patterns of red sand and black shadow. Tibet might be the roof of the world, but Sossusvlei felt like the roof of Mars.

A couple of days later I was struggling with another unfeasibly large geological formation and realising that this is an integral pastime for anyone travelling through Namibia. My guidebook claimed Fish River Canyon was second in size only to the Grand Canyon. A more reliable source in the shape of Gerald, a passing tour leader, said Ethiopia's Blue Nile Gorge was in fact deeper. Either way, the 536m-deep chasm I was trying to climb down was big enough and, just like the sand dunes of Sossusvlei, brilliantly free from coach tours and commercialism. Not for the first time, I felt totally at the mercy of the elements. I'd started my hike at sunrise, but by 8am the heat was already overwhelming. By the time I reached the bottom I was intensely relieved that I hadn't booked myself onto the 85km hike that takes you from one end of the canyon to the other.

Everyone finds a bit of yin and yang when they travel. In Damascus, for example, the serenity of Umayyad Mosque countered the mayhem of surrounding souks and returned my pulse to normal. In Cambodia, a massage from a blind man eased away the stress of 16 hours on the worst road in Asia. But in Fish River, I found the ultimate yang to my canyon-climbing yin — a jacuzzi.

The natural hot spring of Ai-Ais, bubbling away idyllically at the bottom end of the canyon, is the one thing in the world you need after 17 days of travel through Namibia. The green grasses of the pleasant campsite would have been luxury enough, but to lie in a gently simmering spa and soak away the hard-earned layers of dust and grime is as close to heaven as you can get without breaking any laws. Bareback horse riding along the picture postcard river banks in the company of baboon, springbok and eagle completed the paradise effect.

In a way, the comfort of Ai-Ais was preparation for my return to the civilisation of Namibia's capital, Windhoek. But in another, it was the perfect conclusion to a foray into the wilderness and made civilisation harder to bear. So when I arrived in the incongruously German city with its palm-lined streets and air-conditioned department stores, I didn't behave like a savage, but I didn't like the place either.

In just three weeks away from the rest of the human race, the idea of buying food in a supermarket, sleeping in a bed and crossing roads at traffic lights had become alien. Now I look back fondly on my time in Southern Africa's empty quarter. I even miss the dry, matted hair, the long-life camp food, the smelly feet and the irritating girl that brought the Billy Joel tape. I promised myself that I would return to Namibia within the next five years. It was one of those promises travellers make with good intentions, but have little chance of keeping. Although, as a San bushman saying goes, "Now you come, now you go. When you come again you will never go."

Express r...
to nowhere

by Ed Waller

T he old Moor shuffled out from his ramshackle hut, slowly crouched down on his stick and put his right ear on one of the sun-baked metal tracks that stretched off into the heat haze. Eyes closed, he mumbled to himself as he gently waved a few flies from his face. The crowd, even the goats, fell silent. After a few pregnant minutes he straightened up, held his stick aloft and gave an affirmative yell. At last, the train was coming.

The crowd, who'd spent the last five hours lounging in what little shade the afternoon offered, suddenly came alive. Some shouldered wriggling sacks; others rolled gas stoves and bald tyres up to the track. Children dragged Chinese tea chests through the sand on long ropes, and beat scarred donkeys into activity. Vendors flourished groundnuts, pre-historic strawberry creams and fly-clad croissants as they wove through the mass.

Everybody was competing for one of the train's few seats. Fingers twitched on baggage handles and expectant passengers eyed each other nervously, jockeying for the best position. Others just squinted towards the southern horizon, holding up pieces of cardboard to hide their faces from the sun. Only the young Arab, who'd been selling pot-shots on his rifle, leaned back in the shade, happy that the long delay had boosted the day's kings. I peered into the dusty distance — all I could see were the twin silver tracks disappearing into the horizon.

Mauritania's iron-ore train is certainly no Orient Express. Owned by the Société Nationale Industrielle et Minière, this two-and-a-half kilometre succession of open-top ore wagons slowly shunts the 700km between the huge silos on the Atlantic coast and the mines of Zouerat, deep in the Sahara Desert. Each day the four engine cars drag 220 wagons and about 22,000 tons of iron ore. But on the end of this rusting metal giant, the world's longest and heaviest train, is one tiny passenger carriage.

A smudge of dust appeared far to the south and look-outs on the dunes started shouting to their families below. The dust cloud became a twister, snaking its way towards us, and what started as a wind-distorted clatter turned into shrieks of tormented steel as the over-worked brakes tried their best to slow the train. Roaring like a dragon, the locomotive slowly loomed through the swirling dust.

Wagon after wagon lumbered past, and as one we surged forward to the empty carriage. "*C'est la guerre encore,*" muttered a tall Senegali man, who struggled under several plastic sacks and a bucket of wet fish topped with a damp cloth. "*Puis, la bonhomie,*" replied Pahar the elderly Berber, with whom I'd been swapping brioche and CSE French for the past few hours.

Long before the locomotive oozed to a standstill, folk began climbing the huge bogies and hurling themselves into the dusty, shadeless ore wagons, thus saving the 1,000 ougiya (£2.80) fare. Hanging from door handles and hinges, they swamped the passenger carriage long before it finally ground to a halt before me. I now faced a dilemma: whether to climb on to the baking roof and endure the sun and wind, or to gamble everything on a full-frontal assault on the carriage door. Having a hands-free rucksack put me somewhere at the top of the food chain, but my chances of sitting comfortably for the next 20 hours fell sharply after the Senegali, who had sacks in both hands, begged me to carry his bucket.

Somehow, I secured a bridgehead through the surging sea of humans, and my foot found one of the rickety steps to the door. Once I'd got a critical mass of people behind me, I was squeezed through the door like a bar of soap and emerged, somewhat bewildered, within.

I found myself in a long, unlit metal box with two narrow benches running along each side. It was dark, filthy and smelly — fit only for the transportation of cattle. I immediately staked a claim on two yards of bench but soon realised I'd lost not only Pahar my brioche buddy, but also the bucket. I made a decision some might call foolish; I re-entered the mêlée.

The tide of humans, bags, tyres, and stoves threatened to overwhelm me, but in the distance I spied Pahar's fake Nike holdall sinking in the crush immediately outside the door. I lunged at a handle and pulled, on the assumption that he was on the other end. I was kneed in the ribs, I grazed my shin and scuffed my knuckles but eventually dragged the old man, still chewing brioche, onto the bench next to me.

Pahar sat blinking, surprised I'd got such a good position. I spotted the Senegali on the bench opposite, reunited with his fish and grinning with gratitude. With all the benches taken, latecomers nestled where they could. Feet dangled over us from distinctly unsturdy racks. Some lay flat out beneath benches, and the floor space became the new battleground.

Then the women arrived, brightly coloured in tie-dye gossamer gowns. Many were light-skinned Bidan Moors, the slave-owning descendants of warriors. They were enormous, deliberately fattened by their mothers on a rich diet of camels' milk and groundnuts. Ruthlessly, they laid their blankets over the peeling lino, shoving feet and bags aside and marking their territory with cold-blooded efficiency. Blankets laid by one were thrown aside by another who lay her own, only to be usurped by a third.

The space between the benches became a sea of vivid orange and green as the women squeezed between the two lines of seated men. Still people came, cramming all manner of stuff through the tiny windows. As the Blanket Wars raged on, the thirsty sparked up stoves and began brewing tea. Just as some sort of order was finally reached, the train wrenched itself into motion with a loud bang, throwing humans and stoves into turmoil. These chaotic jolts were the modus operandi for the whole journey and I lost count of the number of times I was doused in hot, if fragrant, tea.

Despite the occasional skirmish, the carriage settled down and the mood changed, as Pahar said it would. Spirited conversations sprang up between strangers. As well as tea, apples and bread were shared around. Chipped enamel bowls of *gouvio*, a mixture of camels' milk, sugar and water, were slurped and passed on. Exhausted breasts were unveiled and offered to chubby, snot-encrusted babes. Pahar kept a stash of groundnuts in a battered British Army munitions box, which he rationed out at regular intervals. I incited a small riot by unleashing fresh apricots and, after thrusting them into the nearest grasping hand, never saw them again. In

return, I was handed a baguette lined with camel meat in jambo sauce —
summing up the country's blend of French, Arab and African cuisine.

Our feast was interrupted by the appearance of the ticket inspector,
who carried all his paraphernalia around in a battered cardboard suitcase.
Whenever he and his armed guard ventured through the crush, fare-
dodging women buried themselves beneath the bundle of blankets and
gowns between the benches. Men would hide behind tea chests in the
luggage racks and have to be gently persuaded into paying their fare by the
inspector's burly henchman.

We skirted round the north-western port of Nouâdhibou, Mauritania's
second biggest city. It's an isolated place: halfway along a narrow sand spit
sticking 35km into the Atlantic, this city of 45,000 souls has no permanent
roads linking it to anywhere. Apart from the train, the only ways to reach
Nouâdhibou by land involve lengthy 4WD odysseys south from Fort
Guergarrat in Morocco or north from Mauritania's capital, Nouakchott.

As if this wasn't enough, Nouâdhibou is totally surrounded by
landmines left over from a dispute with Morocco over Western Sahara,
long since forgotten by the West. On the south side of the train track is the
bustling market town; to the north is the deadly silence of the minefields.
These continue east for 400km, hugging Mauritania's northern border and
the route of the train I was travelling on.

Despite its isolation, Nouâdhibou is hectic. Traffic jams of rusty Renault
12s form behind sauntering donkeys and goats, all seemingly deaf to the
hoots of car horns. The market hums with flies attracted to stalls piled with
entrails and goat skins, stuffed with sticky date flesh and sewn up with the
beast's own gut. Tobacco lies spread out on sheets drying in the sun, and
bakers' sons stand patiently with wheelbarrows full of baguettes and
croissants. Women's kaleidoscopic batik, *kente* and mud-cloth gowns clash
with *grande boubous*, the electric blue robes embroidered with gold that most
Moorish men wear. Hand-painted signs denote coiffeurs, pharmacies and
boulangeries, and crunching under every step are sun-bleached sea-shells.

The iron-ore disgorged at the nearby silos provides half of
Mauritania's total exports; fish provides most of the rest. Nouâdhibou's
fishing port is a crowded shanty town called Tcherka, once a settlement for
Canary Islanders. Every afternoon dozens of brightly-painted wooden
fishing boats return, and are dragged up the sand by teams of men who fill
the air with industrious chanting. The day's catch is unloaded from salt

boxes and sold there and then. Donkey carts and pick-up trucks brimming with bleeding fish shuttle between the port and the town centre. Often you see old women dragging huge fish home through the dusty streets, fingers buried to the knuckle in their eye sockets.

As the train left Nouâdhibou behind, the desert turned into a showcase for all the discarded rubbish that the dunes were in the process of digesting. Goats grazed in vast fields of rusting tins and broken brown glass. Fluttering noisily around their hooves were streams of wind-shredded polythene, half buried in the sand, and long tendrils of magnetic tape, no doubt from the low-budget kung-fu videos whose faded posters grace Nouâdhibou's shop walls.

The passengers were now in post-prandial mood, and those who could afford Gauloises offered them round, throwing packets from one end of the carriage to the other. Those who couldn't, smoked local tobacco through ornate *tobah* pipes, finely crafted from copper, ebony and camel bone, which they kept in painted leather pouches. And those who couldn't afford tobahs took occasional puffs on hollowed-out bones, one of which Pahar regularly extracted from deep within his grande boubou. Through the fumes I could see a sign on the wall, pathetically insisting in French, German, Spanish and Russian that we were in a no smoking carriage. In dark corners, animated card games had begun, but Pahar had a life story to tell and I was a keen listener.

"*Je suis Polisario*," he began, proudly. He told me how, in the mid-70s, Mauritania and Morocco tried to carve up the Western Sahara, as if it happened yesterday. And how the indigenous Sahrawi people like him formed a guerrilla army, the Polisario, with Cuban, Libyan and Algerian help. "Fidel, Gadaffi, Bendjedid," the old man muttered, as if they were old friends. Pahar and his kin spent most of the 80s laying mines and blowing up railway tracks. Since then, he'd languished in a refugee camp on the Algerian border, along with the rest of the Sahrawi.

Pahar also asked if I was hoping to enter Morocco illegally. He suggested a good place for me to jump off the train and even said he would guide me safely through the minefields for 1,000 French francs. He looked as though he knew the Sahara like the back of his gnarled hands, but I declined as politely as I could.

Pahar later reached into his boubou and pulled out a small rock, worn smooth with use. With authority, he cleared a space in front of the east-facing window and began rubbing his face and hands with it. Eschewing the mats used in other Islamic countries, Mauritanians rub sand on their faces and forearms while kneeling in prayer, and use such rocks while indoors or on the move. Afterwards, he passed the rock to whoever wanted it, and the carriage filled with the solemn mumblings of the faithful, with many reading aloud from dog-eared Korans.

As the sun set, plastic water bottles were expertly converted into candle lamps and hung from the rafters. Swinging wildly with the train's motion, they gave the impression that we were in the bowels of a wind-swept galleon. The failing sun also meant another session with the prayer stone and people lined up facing the window, as before. Pahar immediately began barking orders and manoeuvring everybody round. The old soldier knew the train had changed direction since the last prayer, and east was now lengthways along the carriage.

With religious duties done, a good old Mauritanian knees-up ensued. The religious chanting evolved into singing, with different ends of the carriage competing on volume. Water containers, now half empty and more resonant, became drums and strange rhythms were tapped out on stoves. Complex follow-me clapping games sprang up, and rainbow-coloured woman danced in the candlelight, their arms held aloft. Amid all this merriment, unless I was very much mistaken, one of the women camped on the floor started playing footsie with me.

I footsied back and was rewarded with a ripple of giggles from the darkness. After a few more such exchanges, a torch went on, illuminating a young woman's face from below. Strange shadows made her face monstrous, and she had badly decaying teeth. I remembered her as one of the ring-leaders in the Apricot Riots.

"Who do you prefer," she asked, forcefully in English. "Pink Floyd or Rod Stewart?" I opted for Floyd, which went down well, and began a debate about British rock bands from the 70s. "When you and I are married," she informed me. "We shall have lots of children. Maybe 20." I tried to haggle her down to a more reasonable figure, but when it became apparent that I wasn't as serious as she was, the torch abruptly went out and there was no more footsie.

Another of the train's excruciating halts signalled our arrival in somewhere called Choum. We'd already stopped at various seemingly random points in the desert, each time depositing a few brave passengers to wander off to some distant tent, but Choum caused the largest flurry of activity. Thick army greatcoats were conjured up, faces were swathed in long cloths, and several men donned industrial goggles to protect themselves from the harsh sand-laced wind outside.

The carriage was emptying and soon the only people left onboard were those going to the mining town of Zouerat. Suitably wrapped, I ventured over to the door that wouldn't shut and experimented, unsuccessfully, with my tobah. Alongside us was another of the mining company's huge steel monsters, stretching silently into the starlit desert in both directions as far as the eye could see.

Choum turned out to be a small collection of railway sheds, home to nothing and nobody. A gaggle of geriatric Peugeot 504s, the workhorses of West Africa, eventually arrived to ferry people to the nearby city of Atar, high on the Adrar plateau. But from the fact that passengers were settling under the bellies of the two trains, I guessed we were in for a long wait and as I relaxed, my mind began to wander.

In the week before I boarded the train I'd taken many a pick-up ride through the Adrar region. I've fond memories of a five-hour, 18-in-a-Land Rover night ride to Atar over steep dunes and boulders. Or there was the four hours I spent with 13 old men in a sweaty Renault 4, the roof of which had been peeled off like a sardine tin. Then there was the bush ambulance hitch from Terjit, shared with an old and dying Moor who whooped like a schoolboy playing Red Indians with every painful pothole.

My personal favourite was the luxurious ride I'd taken from Atar to the ancient city of Chinguetti, when I had the back of a Land Cruiser all to myself. I remembered Atar's noisy fruit market, receding into the dust; hordes of jubilant school children chasing after the jeep, waving their wooden writing boards with glee; the shattered mesas of the Amogar Gorge; a glorious Mauritanian sunset and the desert's grand finale, the endless array of stars.

We stopped twice during that journey; the first time for the toilet — the Africans squatted in a line while this stupid European stood in the wind. The second time, the European squatted with the Africans and began his ablutions, only to find they were praying.

Chinguetti was dark and silent when we finally arrived. Camara, the driver, invited me to stay in his house for a few days, and within minutes I was sharing couscous and macaroni from a huge copper bowl with his family and friends Bounama and Mbodj. While Camara was traditionally dressed, his friends sported the latest in shell suits. My hosts ensured that the best cuts of the goat, such as its liver, were left in my quarter of the dish. All three men were doctors in the local medical centre so our meal was regularly interrupted by villagers bearing poorly children.

In Mauritania, no tea is drunk without ceremony, but that evening I witnessed the full extended tea ritual, courtesy of Mrs Camara. She began the long process with "*bismillah*". The dented pot was then loaded with green Chinese tea and boiled. One glass was poured and the pot was left to boil again. She then decanted the first glass from great heights between the five other glasses until a thick mousse developed in the bottom of each one. The original glass was now discarded, used only as a reservoir for creating more mousse. She then rinsed the outsides of the foam-filled glasses, while somehow retaining their mousse within, and treated them to a tiny measure of new, sweeter tea from the pot. Half an inch of tea beneath three inches of foam. After three mandatory doses of what locals enjoy calling Mauritanian champagne, I was just as thirsty as before.

I awoke next morning with flies crawling up my nose, to a breakfast of dry baguettes and mugs of thick maize soup. Once outside I saw Chinguetti, Islam's seventh holiest city, in all its glory. In the 13th century, the village was a vital meeting place for hajji pilgrims and salt caravans thousands of camels long that were bound for the coast. Now it's a tumble-down, sand-swept village of some 5,000 people. Huge sand drifts blanket the village like snow, piling up against walls and filling the gaps between huts. A victim of shifting trade routes, Chinguetti has been left stranded in the Sahara sand.

Camara's hut was similar to the others: a single-storey, mud-brick dwelling with a low-walled enclosure. Some had grass huts or tents within these walls, but the toilet arrangements were all similar: one would climb on to the designated hut and, in full view of passing villagers, crap through a hole in the roof.

There's also a date grove and an oasis with dozens of cranes for drawing water up from deep wells, which nodded amicably as Bounama and I walked past. Children followed us everywhere, wheeling toys built from cans tied together with twine.

Across the *wadi* is the old quarter. Time and the hungry dunes have swallowed up most of its 13th century grandeur, leaving only a skeleton of broken roofs and walls emerging eerily through the sand. Beyond that, a curvaceous wilderness stretches in every direction, painfully white at noon but luminous orange, copper and cinnamon at sunset.

Bounama spent the next few days introducing me to most of the village, with whom I shared gouvio and tea in a variety of well-carpeted huts. We spent afternoons in the shade of a tree whose thorns are the village's source of toothpicks, playing *damyah*, a local game similar to drafts. The 'board' is a convenient patch of sand, upon which a complicated array of squares and diagonals are drawn. The pieces — sticks of straw for white, balls of dry camel dung for black — are planted where the lines cross.

Another ritual I was first introduced to under that tree is the extended greeting process which Mauritanians embark upon whenever they meet. A lengthy exchange of short, rapidly uttered *bon mots* precede the conversation proper and if any would-be converser doesn't play this game long enough, umbrage is taken. Chinguetti folk also have a habit of emitting clicks from somewhere behind their noses, which I never really got to the bottom of.

Most evenings we watched communal televisions, with extended family and neighbours, until the electricity would abruptly run out and scarab beetles would scuttle about. While listening to a transistor late one night with cousin Dida, Bounama told us about Nouâdhibou's nightclubs and his many evenings spent dancing till dawn. "*Toute musique — samba, Senegalese,*" he enthused, "techno…" This impressed Dida no end, and I realised I was encroaching on Bounama's chat-up routine. "I am also a doctor of the night," he whispered to me with a wink, as I said goodnight.

With Bounama trying his luck with Dida, and the rest of the village asleep, I crept out of the hut and wandered into the surrounding desert. The only sounds were the cicadas and the sporadic complaints of goats. From the comfort of the nearest dune I surveyed the tremendous night sky and began building my own constellations. I got as far as the Triangle and the Great Oblong when it happened — my Africa Moment. Every visitor to this uncompromising cradle of a continent has one — a vague ancestral memory of running around the Rift Valley worrying antelopes. With my back on the Sahara sand, still warm from the sun, and shooting stars erupting above me, I had mine.

Even days later the memories were still strong, but I was suddenly dragged back to the present by a loud bang. The sleepy train lurched forward and Choum retreated into the moonlight. The carriage, a riot of colour and noise only a few hours ago, was now silent. The singing women had gone, the candles had long since flickered out and now the only light came from the dancing orange glow of the occasional Gauloise. Pahar had stretched out on the bench so I sat by the open door with my feet dangling over the edge, watching the flicker of distant nomad fires. The mountains swallowed the moon, the stars went out and an orange glow to the east signalled a new day.

The cold sun revealed mountains, and the train flowed like a glacier as the locomotives strained to drag thousands of tons of stubborn steel uphill. The few remaining passengers began to wake, and some kick-started the tea-making process once more. But the revelry of last night seemed long forgotten — this was another day and there was work to be done. On either side of us the rocky mountains resembled giant slag heaps, rich red with iron. Mauritania's highest peak, Kediet Ijill — the Iron Mountain — blocked out the low morning sun for a while, but soon it was as hot as ever.

Zouerat arrived. Predatory pick-up drivers lay in wait to take people to what is little more than a compound for mine employees and their families. The passengers climbed down from the carriage and traipsed off to work deep underground. Pahar and I wordlessly hugged each other farewell and he too trudged off, munitions box in hand and bone pipe in mouth, to continue his long journey to the refugee camps of Tindouf.

I'd reached the end of the line. Before me lay the mighty Sahara, and desolate dunes stretched eastwards for the next 5,000km, punctuated only by Algeria's Hoggar Mountains and Lake Nasser in Egypt. Prehistoric daubings on ancient cave walls hint that this area once boasted verdant pastures and teeming lakes. All that remain are the huge underground salt deposits to the east that provide Tuareg nomads with a currency once more valuable than gold, but now worth about 100 ougiya (28p) a kilogram from the market.

There was nothing for me to do but wait for the next train back to Choum. "Soon," grinned the toothless ticket-seller, "maybe six hours." He took my crisp 500 ougiya note and gave me a filthy 100 in three separate pieces. "Maybe ten."

Journey into
the Red Zone

by Mark Eveleigh

"**F**ifteen of them," nodded the old hunter. "Hiding by the river — waiting for somebody." He shrugged his wiry shoulders with the nonchalance of a man who had seen more than his fair share of bush bandits. Besides, there was nothing for him to worry about. It was me and my backpack full of Western 'treasures' that they were after. Straining our eyes, we looked past the emerald patchwork of rice paddies, across the muddy sweep of the Manambolo River and into the shadows of the trees. Nothing stirred in the midday heat of western Madagascar.

My would-be ambushers were a bandit tribe known as the Dahalo, who looked like they were set to make my trek through the lawless region of the Zone Rouge more of an adventure than I had bargained for. I weighed up the options. The only transport out of the Zone Rouge, a single bush-taxi, was a week's slog back across a formidable chain of hump-backed ridges and deep, forested ravines. In front of us were the Dahalo and at least five more days of sparsely populated savannah and the craggy Bungolava peaks before civilisation of a sort at Ankavandra, an island in the wilderness boasting three or four satellite hamlets linked by a few miles of dirt track.

"How's he know they're waiting for someone?" I asked my guide.

"He says they were preparing magic," Eloi translated for me, his forehead furrowed with what I considered to be a healthy concern.

In a country where daily life is governed by supernatural powers, magic is not something to be dismissed lightly. Eloi, a devout Catholic and the son of a doctor, again warned me about the Dahalo's powers. "They are more than just bandit thugs," he said. "They have their own magic and carry charms that protect them. If you try to shoot a Dahalo, all he has to say is '*rano*' (water) and your bullets will turn to rain."

Sorcery is a complex affair in Madagascar, and for charms to work the wearer must obey a certain set of taboos: "The Dahalo are not allowed to eat hedgehog or sheep or any other cowardly animal," Eloi continued. "And, above all, they must never, ever wash their shirts."

He was warming to his subject. "You can recognise a real Dahalo because his shirt is yellow with dirt and his eyes are bright red."

I was heading west on a quest that had started as a pipe dream long before I had even heard of the Zone Rouge. I was on the trail of a mysterious tribe of white pygmies known as the Vazimba.

Many Malagasy believe the Vazimba were the indigenous peoples of the island, and some still actively worship them as the most ancient of the ancestors. Malagasy folklore has it that these pygmies (who some claim to be both telepathic and invisible) still exist in hideouts in the western mountains and the region into which they supposedly disappeared is as mysterious as the 'lost tribe' itself.

In remote areas of Madagascar there are few options left to a wayfarer who wishes to travel through the countryside rather than fly over it. In these remote western hills there is only one. So, at Tsiroanomandidy, where the potholes of the grandly named Route Nationale 1 finally crumble into a muddy dirt track, before fading away altogether into the tall grasses of the savannah, I made plans to set out on foot.

My guidebooks were absolutely blank for the entire region that I wanted to cross, from the central highlands to the west coast — an area roughly the same size as El Salvador. Amongst the talkative local stall holders and the noisy backpacker dives of Antananarivo, the island's capital, nobody I'd met had even been as far as Tsiroanomandidy.

But from the moment the Peugeot pick-up bush-taxi finally skidded to a halt in the dusty central square of Tsiro, as the town is known locally, everyone I spoke to was bursting to tell me about the Zone Rouge. Before looking for a room, I stopped to cut the road dust with a bottle of THB (Three Horses Beer) and the barman shocked me with his horror stories of cattle-rustling, murder and torched villages. I tried for a second opinion at the police station, where a macabre desk sergeant added other perils — including kidnapping, slavery and black magic — to the list. I had the impression that Tsiro's boys in blue were not shy about pointing out to a *vazaha* — a foreigner — that they were fearlessly engaged in a crusade against all the combined forces of darkness.

The army had established lonely military posts of three to five men in outlying villages and had even made several helicopter raids into the centre of the Zone Rouge. But the bandits knew the terrain and were forewarned and hidden by villages that were believed to be under their protection. Their leaders, brigands with names like Ratsibahaka ('The Bad Lemur') and Zaza Mola ('Crazy Baby'), were famed for the weapons they carried. It was rumoured that, in the early 80s, the South African Government or the CIA (or both) had supplied some bandit groups with automatic rifles in an attempt to destabilise the socialist government. Yet the bandits were never revolutionaries or guerrillas: they survived primarily by enforcing terror and their own ruthless brand of cattle-rustling.

Madagascar's human population has only recently equalled that of the cattle, and zebu are still the life-blood of the country. Amongst most of Madagascar's 18 tribes a man's worth is still counted in head of cattle. Every week hundreds of hump-backed beasts are herded from the pastures on the western plains to the island's biggest cattle market at Tsiro. This cattle market — lying about 150 miles west of the capital (six hours by bush-taxi) — is the *raison d'être* of the Zone Rouge.

I found a room by the marketplace, where the landlady, Tiana, took advantage of a rare chance to practise her English. She agreed to guide me to the dust bowl on the edge of town where cowboys, dressed in the ubiquitous sarong-like *lambas,* leaned on their spears and watched over their footsore zebu.

"People are moving into Tsiro all the time," Tiana told me. "It's too dangerous to live in the country anymore. The men who bring their cattle to the market often have to fight to get them here and some are killed on the trail." As soon as they'd sold their animals and had money in their pockets the cowboys would be jumping on a bush-hopper back to their villages in the far west. I was unable to tempt anybody into making the return trek across the Zone Rouge.

Just as I was beginning to despair of ever finding a guide who could lead me west I met Eloi Razafimandimby. He had the coffee-coloured good looks and powerful build of the Betsileo tribe, coupled with a deep love for his island and a determination to see as much of it as possible. Formerly a schoolteacher in an isolated Zone Rouge village, he showed an immediate interest in my quest for the Vazimba.

"It could be dangerous if you were alone," he shrugged. "But I know many people there. They won't hurt you if you're with me."

These were the first positive comments I had heard since I arrived in the west and I latched onto them. It wasn't until we were already entering the Zone Rouge — and Eloi began strapping himself into what he called a "homemade bulletproof vest" — that I began to question the wisdom of my decision.

The inhabitants of the few remaining villages in the Zone Rouge live hard lives, tending their paddy fields and herding their precious zebu. Their days are governed by omens and taboos, and their nights by fear of massacre at the hands of the bandits. Sometimes the bandits would send a message advising when they would attack, and as long as the villagers left their cattle when they escaped into the forests there would be no killings. At other times the Dahalo came in the night, without warning or mercy.

Although the settlers came from several of the island's tribes, they were firmly united in the pioneer spirit that had brought them to this lawless country where there is an abundance of good, rich land... if you're prepared to fight for it.

In the settlements along the way the headmen would give us spears to keep next to our sleeping mats, and if the village owned a shotgun they kept an armed guard on patrol throughout the night. Despite the tension, I always felt that I was among friends in these hamlets. On one occasion I fell peacefully asleep under the gaze of five young men, who leaned on their spears watching over the first vazaha who had ever been in their village.

Often there was nothing to eat but boiled rice and a handful of peanuts, yet the villagers were always ready to share what they had with a visitor and we'd repay them from the provisions we carried from Tsiro. Meat is rarely eaten except on ceremonial occassions, but twice we were honoured with freshly killed hens. Rice water — laughingly known as whisky Malgache — was the usual beverage and, after being boiled for a couple of minutes with the burnt rice in the pot, was surprisingly tasty and reassuringly sterile.

Most of the homes were made from woven saplings, plastered with zebu dung that had hardened like concrete under the powerful equatorial sun. A ramshackle collection of six of these huts, near the Bungolava mountains, went by the name of Soa Tana ('Sweet Town') and it was here the old hunter warned us about the Dahalo ambush.

We felt nightmarishly vulnerable as we lowered ourselves into the swirling coffee-coloured Manambolo River. The sun was just climbing over the hill at our backs and it was still cold when we stepped warily into the shadows under the trees on the opposite bank. We sat still for a few minutes, holding our breath and listening for the crack of twigs underfoot, before scrambling through a wall of giant bamboo and up out of the valley. Then we were in headlong flight, striking directly towards the Bungolava mountains rather than sticking to the infinitely easier, but more predictable, valley trails. We crossed the rolling savannah of Bezavona ('Place of Many Mists') in a single day, such was our determination to leave the bandits behind. That night we camped in a densely wooded gully, shielding the glow of our campfire as best we could.

We added three extra days to our trip by taking the most unpredictable (and therefore ludicrous) route across a seemingly endless chain of hills and valleys, covered with what I was beginning to think of as man-eating grass.

Swaying two metres above our heads, vero grass not only sliced like razorblades, it seriously reduced our already slim chances of successful pygmy-spotting. Furthermore, these vero patches were no more than islands in a sea of grass of a far more vicious nature. Danga grass is crowned with sharp black spines that seep a resin so that it sticks together in a tangled mat. As you drag your legs through this gluey mass, the spines are dislodged by the dozen to go about their business of insinuating themselves slowly but surely into your flesh. I soon began to appreciate why the Dahalo might have been reluctant to follow us.

On top of all this, Eloi was determined to add the blood-guzzling spirit animals of Bungolava to my list of woes.

"The *songaomby*'s like a big sheep, but it lives on the blood of men," he was explaining. "A man from my hometown once tried to hide in a tree when he saw a *songaomby*. This was very silly because everybody knows that it plays a wicked trick to get you down. It stood underneath the tree and it..." — he paused, searching for the *mot juste*. "How you say? It peed, and swished its tail. The pee burns like acid and the man fell out of the tree when he got splashed. The *songaomby* ate him."

My friend shook his head sadly. "Nobody ever saw him again."

Eloi's tribe the Betsileo — 'The Invincibles' — has ancestral homelands on the southern end of the island's central plateau. Although the Betsileo are generally the most widely travelled of Madagascar's tribes, they maintain a deep-rooted horror of dying away from home in case their spirit can't find its way back to the homelands. If a relative who has been buried in a distant land appears in a dream, it is taken as an unmistakable sign that his spirit is restless and feels abandoned. Speedy arrangements must be made to bring him home as soon as possible and at any cost. There are endless sagas of loyal Betsileo trekking for weeks on end with suitcases bearing the remains of wayward loved ones.

In a country as racially diverse as Madagascar, the Betsileo have, to a great extent, retained the characteristics of the island's first settlers, the pioneers who made the long voyage from Indonesia almost 2,000 years ago. These intrepid sailors introduced their highly developed fishing techniques, stilted houses that could withstand the monsoons and the ecologically disastrous slash-and-burn agricultural system that might have been responsible for driving them from their islands to Madagascar in the first place. From the cycle trishaws of the highlands to the *pirogue* outriggers of the west coast, Madagascar still feels much closer to Asia than to Africa.

It was not until centuries later that the first statuesque Bantu cattle-herders crossed the 400km Mozambique Channel from Africa. It occurred to me that they could well have described the short, wiry Indonesians that they found there as 'white pygmies.'

Unfortunately it was nothing to do with his 'invincible' tribal roots that had led Eloi to take off his 'bulletproof vest'. I knew the thick leather straps were excruciatingly uncomfortable. He wasn't yet confident that we were out of the bandits' reach. We didn't realise, as we hauled ourselves over the highest ridge in the Bungolava mountain range, that we were heading towards the main recruiting grounds of the Dahalo. All across the Zone Rouge, gangs of likely lads were heading west towards blood-or-glory at the year's biggest bare-knuckle, street-fighting festival in the town of Antsalova.

"Did I ever tell you about the *kalanoro*?" Eloi began as we scrambled down the western slope of Vatosira Mountain. "He's a little hairy man, his feet point backwards and he can't resist the smell of frying pistachio nuts..."

Sorcerer bandits, killer grass, man-eating sheep, and now hairy, pistachio-craving dwarfs. It seemed that even the helpful desk sergeant in Tsiroanomandidy had understated the facts when he warned me about what I might be letting myself in for in the Zone Rouge.

My ankles were painfully poisoned by danga thorns by the time we splashed through the paddy fields surrounding the wilderness town of Tsiandro. I tried not to think about the likelihood of the muddy water being infected with bilharzia as I stopped to savour its delicious coolness.

Tsiandro lies close to the northern end of the Tsingy de Bemaraha Reserve. Gaston, the local warden and by proxy the district *délégué* or government representative, showed us to a room in the official compound.

"Everything that arrives in Tsiandro must be carried here on a man's back, for two days," said Gaston, explaining why the half-dozen bottles of Three Horses Beer that had just been rustled up were the most expensive I'd yet bought in Madagascar. "Not only that, but most people here don't use money at all. For instance," — some words of Malagasy were rattled off between himself and the ever-present crowd of children blocking the doorway — "at current exchange rates, a jar of sugar equals three of rice, and a bottle of THB equals eight jars of rice."

Gaston was a mine of information on everything to do with the area and he set us up not only with a knowledgeable guide to lead us through the dense forests of the reserve, but also with a lead on the Vazimba pygmies. A few hours' walk to the north-west, he told us, there was a tiny village, the headman of which was said to be Vazimba.

George, our new guide, appeared early the next morning wearing a skirt of bright orange plastic. "To keep out the danga," he winked.

We stocked up on rice and coffee and tramped out of Tsiandro with George swinging a live hen for fresh meat during our three-day crossing of the reserve. The towering limestone pinnacles of the Tsingy, Madagascar's most famous geological feature, lie mostly at the southern end of the national park and very few tourists ever visit this northern section.

Although most of Madagascar's lemurs are to be found in the few pockets of rainforest that remain in the east, George was soon pointing out groups of magnificent, woolly Verreaux's sifaka. They looked strangely human staring down at us from the highest treetops, with their black skullcaps and snowy fur coats.

Chameleons were everywhere and I saw more snakes in our trek through the Tsingy de Bemaraha than I've seen over several months in other tropical countries. My pleasure at seeing these creatures was further enhanced by the knowledge that there are no poisonous land snakes in Madagascar.

George was full of information about the creatures of Bemaraha, though some of their habits were hard to believe. "There's a snake called *fandrefiala* that lives in the reserve. It's rare, but very dangerous. It has a poisoned spear-tip for a head and will drop out of the trees to kill anybody who walks underneath." Both of my guides were clearly convinced of the existence of these beasts, and I did my best never to show my scepticism.

George and Eloi were still describing Madagascar's weird and wonderful creatures as they led me limping into a dusty square between a collection of rickety huts. Two men came smilingly forward. One was tall and lanky, the other short and bandy-legged, but they were both dressed in the shorts and T-shirts that are now the dress of choice across most of the country. A teenager appeared, firing off a volley of cheerful French: "*Bienvenue, m'ssieurs. Comment allez vous?*" With his lamba worn toga-like over one shoulder and a large plastic comb stuck in his hair (the badge of a Malagasy dandy) he appeared to be the traditionalist in this motley group.

One by one they stepped forward to offer the formal two-handed handshake. None would have dreamt of betraying bad manners by letting us see that we had not been expected. At first it had been unnerving to think that our arrival was so obviously anticipated in these wilderness hamlets and I'd assumed that the bush telegraph had travelled ahead, as it almost always does. But as we moved onto remoter and more untrodden trails I realised that this was impossible. Even in the most isolated communities it was regarded as simple good manners to greet us like old friends who had just popped over from a neighbouring village.

An old man came out of a hut, screwing his eyes up against the sun. I wondered if we had interrupted his siesta. Mahatoky could have been 70, though was probably not much older than 50, and was the headman of this modest collection of seven huts that was bestowed with the impressive name — even by Malagasy standards — of Ankazomandiladongo. He was dark-skinned, with finely chiselled features and he wore a ragged denim jacket on the back of which somebody, in another lifetime, had painstakingly embroidered 'Harley Davidson'.

At just under five feet, Mahatoky might have qualified for the textbook definition of a pygmy if it weren't for the fact, as he explained later, that all Vazimba were not created equal. He had a disconcerting way of smilingly redirecting my questions so that I had the impression that he preferred to guide me into answering them for myself. I asked Mahatoky what he could tell me about the Vazimba and he showed us to some low stools in the lengthening shadow of his hut.

"This is not my own lie," he began, using the traditional disclaimer with which any self-respecting old-time Malagasy sage would have started his tale, "this is a lie that the ancestors told me."

He massaged his salt-and-pepper beard while the teenage dandy filled some enamel cups with delicious sugar cane wine, then he leaned forward to tell me the story of the Vazimbas' arrival in the west.

"At the time when the Merina tribe defeated the Vazimba and drove us from our highland capital, near where Antananarivo stands today, we had a great king called Andrianavaovao. He led his people westwards from the Massif Central, across the Bungolava Mountains to the Manambolo River."

He paused and cast a peaceful eye over the village with the air of an old man who could no longer see any reason to hurry. "The King's sister Ampelamana was also a great leader, but she had a son who was bad. Betandra, the son, was in love with one of his uncle's wives. He wanted to kill the King but Andrianavaovao got to hear of the treachery, and he killed the young man with the knife that was meant for himself."

Mahatoky leaned back against the wall of the hut and remained silent for so long that I began to wonder if he was going to continue. Only when our cups had been refilled with the sweet wine did he break his silence.

"Words are like rice plants," he said. "They must be carefully arranged... and watered. Ampelamana, heartbroken by the death of her only son and tired of the journey, decided to settle her followers in the Manambolo valley. They became Vazimba Andrano ('Vazimba of the Waters'), and very soon their blood was lost among the people of the long valleys. Our king continued the trek with his wives and subjects — along the trail by which you came here — and finally they stopped to plant their rice and raise their zebu in this area. They became the Vazimba Antety — the 'Vazimba of the Plateau'.

"I'm the last Vazimba Antety," Mahatoky sighed. "Everybody else here is Sakalava, from the valleys, and my children are Sakalava-Vazimba."

"When did all this happen?" I asked. "How many generations ago?"

"It's impossible to say," came Eloi's translated answer. "Monsieur Mahatoky says the story's always been this way."

This wasn't unusual. Until French colonisation rural Malagasy did not recognise any time structure beyond agricultural cycles and specific obligations relating to loyalty to the ancestors. But there was something else that I wanted to ask, going back even further in time. Would the old man be able to tell me how the Vazimba first arrived in Madagascar?

"Ask him," I said, "where his people first came from. In other words, what's his belief of the beginning of life?"

Mahatoky waited patiently whilst the question was interpreted and then turned slowly to fix a crooked smile upon me. I'm not saying it was the legendary Vazimba telepathy, but I didn't need a translator to tell me what he was thinking: "Nobody knows that. Did this strange vazaha come all this way to ask me that?"

If only Mahatoky could have known just how far I had travelled to meet him. But how could I explain all this?

I would have liked to stay in Ankazomandiladongo longer, but it wasn't to be. In three more days we would complete our trek through western Madagascar. Eloi was anxious to get back to his fiancée in Tsiro and — what with danga-poisoning and malaria — I was desperately in need of a rest myself. So we shook hands and limped onwards.

We were sat around a riverside campfire that evening chewing on our freshly killed celebratory chicken as the lavender sky blushed to an impossible crimson. As Eloi and I were reflecting on everything that we'd seen in our weeks in the Zone Rouge I remembered an old Malagasy proverb: "It is the destiny of the hen to die at the moments of man's greatest happiness."

The grave men of Malawi

by Juliet Coombe

"**C**ome closer honey, we can't see you," insisted one of the campers, holding a Carlsberg beer in one hand and waving at me with the other. "Jeez, what are you wearing? Are deckchairs the latest London fashion now?" Sure enough, the loudest drinkers in the camp were to be my travelling companions for the next four weeks, and I'd turned up wearing second-hand cast-offs in lurid primary colours.

Trudging through the hot African bush the next day, I asked myself what I was doing. I was sweaty, my feet hurt, I was hungry, and I had the hangover from hell. At least this time a soldier wasn't pointing a machine gun at me and barking orders. When I'd first visited Malawi in 1987, Dr Hastings Kamuzu Banda was in charge of the country. He was known as the 'Grave Man', and not just because of his deadpan seriousness.

During his dictatorial rule many things were outlawed. While I was there I managed to break two of Banda's laws — I had the Lonely Planet guidebook to the continent that accused Banda of being a dictator and a tyrant, and I was wearing trousers which was forbidden for women.

Although not a hanging offence, it meant instant deportation and a two-day walk to the first village in Tanzania. At least I hadn't been carrying a biology book, which according to Banda was pornography and would have meant a spell in a rat-infested prison.

There was no immediate danger of being deported by the fashion police this time, although I was dressed in the sort of outfit I would generally only wear to a fancy dress party. Banda had been replaced by Dr Bakili Muluzi in the first multi-party democracy elections in 1994, and, comparatively speaking, was a liberal. Women were now free to wear trousers if they wanted to. I wanted to, but after spending several hours watching planes being unloaded at Kamuzu airport, about 30km from the capital, Lilongwe, it became clear my bags had taken a very different journey to me.

If I was going to spend the next four weeks in Malawi in more than just the clothes I stood up in then I desperately needed a new wardrobe. Lilongwe market, ten minutes from the old city centre, seemed the obvious place to start. The first stalls I came to at the start of Malangalanga Road were selling gnarled pieces of wood, snakes in bottles of brown coloured water and signs saying, '*Dental, medical or emotional. We help you.*' I needed saving, but I knew bits of old wood rubbed together wasn't going to solve my problems.

Jet lagged, dishevelled and desperate to get something clean on, I walked into the heart of the market. After the stalls of herbs and potions, Malawi women sold all types of colourful fruit, from avocados the size of footballs to big bunches of bananas. A couple of girls made me laugh when I said I needed clothes and they held up two ripe mangoes and danced suggestively. Further into the market, past the paw paw and guava jam stalls, old men sat round exchanging gossip and drinking red and blue cartons of alcoholic *Chibuku*.

Just as I was about to give up and head back into town, I turned a corner and found mountains of second-hand clothes. It was the open-air equivalent of an charity shop. Western clothes in mint condition were muddled together with cheap cast-offs that had been fixed with colourful patches. I rummaged all over the place, but nothing was my size and most items looked like they'd come from a 70s bad taste party. Much of the clothing could have been maternity wear, and, no matter how much the stallholder said the pink, white and blue flowery nylon fabric really suited me, it looked simply hideous. I had visions of walking around looking like I was dressed in a pair of curtains. Still, I needed clothes, and realising that if I was going to lose my dignity I might as well lose it properly, I selected a range of the loudest items I could find.

My aching feet and pounding head brought me back to reality. Where was the beach? Why weren't we driving? I thought overland trips meant trucks. Visions of luxury were disappearing faster than a politician's promise. A few miles in the African bush can seem like a marathon if you are not used to wear walking boots.

We finally reached Kande Beach on Lake Malawi, and all I wanted to do was go to sleep. But no, we had to put up our tents — my least favourite job after being trailer-packer and truck-cleaner. Every time I tried to hammer in a tent peg my head screamed at me to stop. Eventually I was able to relax. I needed food and lots of it.

Bandi Paterson, a local village boy who acted as a guide to pay his way through secondary school, showed me how they turned cassava into flour. One of his friends offered to make banana cake with it for a dollar. By the time I'd put up my tent and cleaned the truck, a stodgy flat yellow cake arrived, smothered in powdery flower and weighing a ton.

Tentatively I pulled off a piece and tried it. Surprisingly, it was delicious, and much better at lining my stomach than the beans and chicken bone soup we had for dinner that night. Sitting around the campfire, Bandi and his friends asked me about my life back home and spoke about their life around the lake. "The lake is our lifeline; we rely on it for food, transport, wate and recreation. And it brings the tourists," explained Bandi as the campfire crackled.

We were woken at 5am and told to pack the tents and get ready for the day-long drive to Nyika Plateau. It was a rude awakening to the reality of overland life. The sun beat down as the truck bounced along the potholed road, covering us in dust. The round huts that I'd seen littering the landscape on my first visit had been replaced by corrugated iron buildings and roughly fired red bricks. The landscape was a patchwork of cotton, banana and tobacco plantations, broken by the occasional baobab tree, root-like branches hung in the air as if a giant had uprooted them.

Before we reached Mzuzu we stopped at a rubber plantation where trees were bled for their sap. One of the tree cutters dripped white sap onto the palm of my hands and said,

"This can be turned into highly durable condoms and rubber tyres, try pulling it and you will see how strong it is."

Sticky fingered and covered with dust, we stopped in Mzuzu to shop for provisions, before beginning the long climb into the mountains. The truck, laden with bags of flour, eggs and other food, huffed and puffed like an unfit climber as it struggled up the twisting mountain road. The long, tiring journey was well worth it. Nyika is Malawi's largest and highest national park, and the rolling hills, plentiful valleys and ravines which support dense green wildlife-packed woodland reminded me in some ways of Scotland.

We were welcomed at the gates to the 1,900-square-kilometre game reserve by women selling pots of delicious golden honey. As the sun finally vanished behind the highest peak and the stars began slowly appearing, we set up camp for the night. Kids of all ages from the Aphoka tribe joined us for our evening meal, laughing at our strange cooking methods.

"What you hunt?" asked one boy pointing at my big grocery bag.

I felt rather lame saying I'd bought everything in the supermarket in Mzuzu. At least it was better than 'what are you wearing?', which was what most people I'd met had asked me.

With what seemed to be a mix of bemusement and embarrassment, they looked away and started to play Bowo, a traditional Malawi board game requiring 32 coffee beans and a great deal of patience. The object of Bowo is to take as many beans from your opponent as possible. As the game progressed, more children from the village joined us and I started to feel like a celebrity as more than 50 pairs of eyes stared at me. One girl in a small top emblazoned with pictures of the Spice Girls stood slightly back from the group. Looking very serious, she warned us about the hyenas.

"The last truck that came through had its headlights and trailer chain chewed through, and the one before lost all its wheel caps," she said gravely.

Shivering in the cold, she moved forward, pushing a couple of the boys out the way. I moved to one side so she could get closer to the fire.

"Be careful of the frosty," she said mysteriously as she warmed herself. Before I could ask her what she meant distant drums echoed across the valley and the Aphoka kids scattered, disappearing into the night.

Hyenas may have been waiting for the chance to chomp on truck headlights, but the orchestra of snoring coming from the camp that night would have put off any animal, no matter how mischievous they were.

The next day was another early start. We were heading to the main camp at Chelinda, 48km into the park. Tragically, due to so many of the animal corridors vanishing under the weight of massive urbanisation across Africa, it is now impossible for certain wildlife to migrate to and from the plateau. Lions were the first to vanish some 20 years ago, but there are still plenty of zebra, eland, reedbuck, roan, leopard and hyenas in the park.

After a few long, hard days on the road we were all excited about the chance to soothe our aching bodies and parched throats with a few drinks at the lodge bar. Unlike the others who had left while there was still some daylight, I foolishly chose to have one more drink and enjoy some home comforts. After all, it was only a short walk back to the campsite. What could go wrong?

A few minutes away from the soft sofas and the cold beers of the lodge a leopard crossed my path, meandering along and minding its own business. I froze. Stupidly I lifted my camera and took a couple of shots. The whirring of the camera shutter caused the cat to stop in its tracks and turn round. It pawed the ground, snarling. I backed away. Ducking into a small ditch, I prayed. Nothing happened. Maybe the thought of tackling somebody wearing a bright orange top and electric green trousers from the Lilongwe market was too much for the leopard.

Continuing through the bush and over the brow of another hill, my heart sank as I realised that I had taken a wrong turn and was lost in the middle of the game reserve. Panic set in. I was in the African bush at night without a torch. It was getting cold and the moon had vanished behind the clouds. I doubled back, trying to work out which way I'd come. As I was wondering how I was going to get myself out of this mess, I noticed a beam of light from the bar over the brow of a hill. Eyes focused firmly on the light, I picked my way through the undergrowth, and before I knew it I was home. At the campsite the others had been preparing to send out a search party. Relieved to be safe, I hugged my coffee and watched the fire. I never thought I would be that pleased to hear the same old campfire conversations about sex.

Apparently the greatest challenge on any overland trip was to have sex in a single camp bed without getting your knees trapped between the metal legs. As the drink continued to flow late into the night and the conversations got raunchier, I pondered the campsite gymnastics they seemed so fond of talking about.

That night, whilst most of us slept and others tried out the latest camp bed ergonomics, the hyenas finally caught up with the truck. One gas pipeline was chewed through, one chrome water bottle was chomped and we were missing a bag of tent pegs and a hammer. I could just picture them sitting on the brow of the hill laughing at their handiwork and the havoc they had created. With no gas, breakfast was an unmitigated disaster. Finally — after some makeshift surgery with tape repaired the gas pipe — we managed to eat, and it didn't even stop us from leaving for Livingstonia and Chitimba camp on time.

The long, mind-numbing drive to Chitimba was only broken 25km north of the Rumphi turn-off for a picnic lunch. We had just under one hour to see the person considered by many to be Malawi's greatest eccentric, Mr SS Ngoma. His home was more than a little weird, made out of scrap metal, old car and truck parts, brightly painted pieces of wood, disused road signs saying '*This way to God*' and stickers left behind by previous visitors.

The red headstone in the far corner of the garden said Mr Ngoma was born in 1913. For a man who had survived two World Wars and Banda's 30-year dictatorial rule which turned Malawi into the world's fourth poorest nation, he was totally obsessed with death — his death. His bizarre house-turned-mausoleum was dedicated to his impending funeral and life in heaven, while also showing signs of once being a highly successful grocery shop. The large slogan stamped into the front of his house saying '*God is love*' was only overshadowed by the even bigger '*Get your groceries here*' sign.

Walking through his elaborate front gate, I half expected to see packed shelves of dusty cans of baked beans left over from the 1950s. For a man whose life was dedicated to death, the white-bearded, 87-year-old Ngoma was surprisingly healthy and agile.

"Come in, come in, God be with you, he loves us all," he said as he energetically waved me in.

He offered to give me a guided tour around his house. During the tour Ngoma would stop explaining bits of his eccentric abode to speak on his mobile phone for a few minutes. Then, turning his attention back to me, he would continue proudly reeling off the history of his country.

"David Livingstone," he said "a Scottish missionary from the 19th century discovered my country and called my people Malavi, which meant, 'reflected light of the lake' and that was later adopted as the present name of the country."

Holding up the phone he said, "David can tell you for himself."

I backed away, unnerved at the thought of having a conversation with a man who died in 1873.

In one well-worn wooden room on the second floor, Ngoma had built his coffin and surrounded it with religious placards. Simple bold, underlined statements slapped over the peeling walls acted as wallpaper; '*The world would be OK if we loved each other*' and '*praise be to the Lord*'. In another room there was a mortuary temple and chapel, complete with a 60s record player and giant speaker wired to the veranda so everyone could hear his hymns and sermons on why we should all follow Jesus.

Shuffling from room to room, he insisted that I listen to a deafening bell attached to the side of his house before we entered the inner sanctum. Here he proudly showed me his gramophone. Luckily, God was not inspired by Ngoma's taste in music and it failed to work. Sitting inside the tiny chapel he pressed the buttons on his phone, and again claimed that it allowed him to speak to God.

Ngoma's tour, however, was far from over. He demonstrated his toilet, a long pipe running from his window, down the side of the house and into his garden. "Piss, piss," he joked, picking up the piece of pipe and waggling it about. Lovingly patting the tube, Ngoma said; "It is a great way to water the garden."

It was time to leave — although not to the higher place that was calling Ngoma. Mount Livinstonia, Malawi's highest mountain was beckoning. Mountain climbs can be testing, but this didn't look difficult. Twenty five kilometres, straight up.

We started our trek from Chitimba, a beach on the shores of Lake Malawi, at 6am. Ahead, pointed out our guide, were 22 hair-raising bends across escarpments and through dense forest. The possibility that this was going to be harder than it looked began to dawn on me.

In the past, climbers could walk along the old Garode Road, which was constructed by missionaries in 1905. Now, bandits from Tanzania slash tourists' faces for dollars and hold tour groups up at gunpoint. The only safe way was to go through the thick undergrowth and hope you did not slip down one of the steep ridges.

"The harder the climb, the safer you are," laughed my cheeky guide as I fell over and caked myself in mud. If walking over gnarled tree stumps and rocky outcrops with terrifying drops wasn't bad enough, it started to rain. First large, gentle drops followed by a torrential downpour. The slippery slopes reduced me to crawling on my hands and knees in places. I cursed myself for taking on the climb, instead of chilling out at Chitimba.

The monsoon lasted for an hour and the conditions totally sapped my strength. Most of my fellow climbers, exhausted by the terrain and appalling weather conditions, had already decided to turn round. A stubborn streak made me even more determined not to be defeated.

Along the way I met mountain families preparing cassava for breakfast and was offered large cups of the local brew to keep me going. The climb took me past several small communities, and at the lower levels simple plots of farming land had been hacked out of the harsh mountainside. As my water supplies started to dwindle we reached the largest of Livingstonia's waterfalls, 50 tumbling metres with a cave behind. A few kilometres on and I rejoined the dirt path that leads to the picturesque village of Livingstonia.

I'd never been so relieved to reach my destination. It had taken four treacherous hours, but the rewards at the top of the mountain made it worthwhile.

In Livingstonia I headed to the Stone House, which has been turned into a museum and simple guesthouse. Outside, overgrown bricks spelt out the biblical reference, *Ephesians 2.14*. My next stop was a Scottish-style church with stained glass windows, those in the portal depicting Livingstone's life. Luckily the chapel was open and I went in, looking for a bible to find out what the reference on the bricks outside meant. I found the relevant passage which read, '*For he is our people who hath made both men and hath broken down the middle wall of partition between us.*'

The vicar approached me as I read the lines over and over again to myself. I asked him what they meant. "The coded biblical message was for all the passing planes, to tell them that no matter what happened to the country the missionaries would stay in Livingstonia, whatever the consequences," he replied.

He showed me round the decaying Victorian church, which had been founded in 1894, and explained the challenges of building a community in those days. "The magnificent stained glass window over the entrance depicts not only Doctor David Livingstone, but also his two faithful companions Juma and Guze, his sextant and medicine chest, with the blue lake acting as a backdrop to the great adventures."

With only a few hours to go before dusk I had to head back down the mountain. Surely this would be easier than the climb. To my surprise it was even harder. With every step I feared slipping and tumbling down the mountain into the lake below.

Back at the camp, footsore, covered in blisters, yet high on adrenalin and still exhilarated by the climb, I managed to find enough energy to pack up my tent. It was time to head for the Karonga border crossing and travel into Tanzania.

My heart was full of dread as we headed for Karonga. I had flashbacks to 1987 when I was thrown out of a police car with my bags and my deportation orders. I had no idea which way to go or how long it would take me to cross the Tanzanian border. As I remembered it, the road to Karonga was hell and left your throat full of dust and grit. Things had changed, now the last 40km of the road were tarmacked. Some things, however, hadn't changed. The immigration office was still the same; a giant grey shed left over from the Cold War era. It even had the same ledgers where you filled in your personal details in longhand. Computers had not reached this northerly crossing; indeed I'm not sure any computer would survive the journey. Even the guards looked the same, albeit 14 years older and wrinklier. My heart skipped a beat — they couldn't be the same ones, surely.

Trembling, I put a scarf round my head as a disguise and made my way into the passport control queue.

One guard joked with an Icelandic girl in front of me that her country was one big fridge freezer. Suddenly it was my turn. I stepped up to the counter. Nervously I handed over my passport. He looked up and his eyes narrowed. "I know you," he said. I shook my head and looked at my feet. He starred at me intently. "Yes," I admitted sheepishly. To my surprise his grimace melted into a huge grin and the exit stamp came down like a judge's gavel.

Walking back into the African sunshine I felt a great relief. It might have been more than a decade on but I was free to finish the trip I had started and leave the country the way I had intended. The lake lay behind me like a twinkling diamond, as our truck headed off for more adventures on the wide-open African plains. Malawi vanished behind a cloud of orangey-brown dust, but my memories were no longer of trauma, only joy and delight.

The Catio roadshow

by Nikita Gulhane

I was startled out of my reverie by a thud on the ground next to me. Gentle vibrations reached my feet and I became aware of a chorus of giggling. A small green fruit rolled against my heel and stopped. The shaking in the branches above gave way to hissed whispers of '*Branco*'. A hand darted out to pick up the fallen mango. Small boys. I pondered two things. Why the entire male population under the age of ten seemed more at home up trees than on the ground? And why I, of Asian descent with clearly brown skin, was referred to as branco — or 'White Man'. The pondering stopped almost as soon as it started when a battered flat-bed truck, carrying a cargo of dusty, smiling people, veered onto the road to Catio and limped to a halt under the mango tree.

There are no truly compelling reasons to visit Catio. It might be Guinea-Bissau's largest town in the south, but that still only means a few thousand people. It's not geared up for tourists and there are certainly no hotels. The town's itinerary of buildings would read as: one telephone transmitter, one generating station powered by two engines from a Second World War Russian warship, one hospital, the Governor's Palace, two schools, one night club with dining facilities, one restaurant (two tables) and a jail. Most young people want to leave for Bissau, it's only the aid agencies who want to stay. Balantes are the dominant tribe, the rest of the population being a mixture of Muslim Fula and Mandinka. Even for many Guineans, Catio is well off the map — it's just too much hassle to get to. I was only visiting because I'd never been to West Africa and had never heard of Guinea-Bissau until a friend came to work here. Come down for May Day, he said. So I did.

A small expectant crowd immediately surged around the truck, offering small bags of peanuts for sale or helping relatives down. The driver leapt from his cab grinning and waving acknowledgement to the cries of "Yarr, Ventura". He shook hands and ruffled the hair of the small boys who had mysteriously melted from the branches to group by his side. Then he strolled over to a cluster of food shacks and flirted a piece of dried fish from one woman and a plastic bag of water from another. He was obviously a local hero, perhaps Guinea-Bissau's answer to Sean Connery. Such style, especially the way he casually strolled round the back of the shacks and pissed into a bush. He returned to the truck and, with a flourish, waved the small boys away. He produced a jack from a roll of oily cloth and started raising the rear axle to change the flat tyre, much to the excitement of those still seated in the back of the truck. Those who had left earlier were by now morphing enigmatically in the heat haze; a shimmering bar code in a sea of red dust gradually shrinking into the horizon.

Ventura dusted his hands on his trousers and started accepting money for places. Old women, like giant leather spiders, hauled themselves up into the back of the truck. Children and livestock were used as putty to seal them in while the young men perched around the edge providing a frame. That just left three club class seats in the cab, the prize for paying a few pesos more — at least there was more money to be made from brancos. Not that this was a serious attempt to upgrade quality; the ripped green vinyl seat coverings made no attempt to hide the hard boards beneath.

The truck heaved itself off the soft sand and lurched down the Catio Road, not so much a road as a chance break in the vegetation. In the rainy season it's a swerving, sliding mucus trail of a track and in the dry, a spine-shattering study in slow torture. The bus journey from the capital Bissau, 160km away, had taken four hours. The next 60 would take another three — and this was the dry season.

As soon as I had crossed the border from Senegal into Guinea-Bissau I couldn't help feeling that I was travelling through a film set. The villages we passed revealed an existence I had read about in geography lessons more than 20 years ago: women sifting rice, bare-breasted girls ferrying wood on their heads or grooming babies, and men sheltering under trees. It was too good to be true, and the voyeur in me thrilled to the thought that I was witnessing something powerful, something truly African. OK, so these were clichés, the kind of nonsense that comes from being a Westerner with the freedom to travel. But there were also a few niggling doubts about being in a country where I was so obviously an outsider. We all carry our psychological baggage and, as a Brit born of Asian parents, mine had more compartments than most.

We juddered down the track. The sweat from my thighs was sending me sliding between the windscreen and gearbox. Every now and then shrieks of laughter would carry across from the back as a tendril of vegetation slapped someone's face. From the relative safety of the cab the outside world was complete chaos. Plant warfare. No order, no nothing, just rampant lush vegetation, massive mahoganies, palm trees with their crown of bright red nuts and the occasional stumpy, pot-bellied baobab. Up north the land is thin scrub, with neat plantations of groundnuts or mangoes lining the highway. The roadside villages are crowded with market stalls, some with shops — I even saw a battered petrol pump. Down south it's different. Here the jungle rules.

Ventura mumbled something in Crioulu and then discharged an impressive stream of saliva and chewed kola nut out of the window. Sixty kilometres is not very long as far as road trips go, but I was grateful for the several stops we made at tiny hamlets, sometimes with only two or three low thatched huts. What were people doing out here? How did they survive? Our arrival was always greeted with a great deal of excitement. Ventura would hoot his horn and skid the truck to a halt. Hands appeared through the red dust, waving and high-fiving. As huge bundles of possessions were passed down, those staying on took their chance to stand up in the back and banter with the locals. All the while thin raised arms holding small bunches of stubby green bananas for sale circulated around the truck. Only by leaning out of the window could you see the small grinning children attached.

The last few miles to Catio were on metalled road. Perhaps one day the whole route would be covered, and an African experience — albeit a fairly torrid one — would be lost. My friend came to meet me at the bus stop. I could feel my presence creating an immediate stir. Visitors were rare and I certainly didn't fit the accepted view of a branco. Curious glances accompanied us as we walked from the bus to his hut. Shadowy figures stared out from the dark interior of their huts. And all the while the hot sand burned my feet through the gaps in my sandals. I wondered if they had ever seen an Asian before. Would they even know I was Asian? I later met a man who'd never seen a white face until Cuban soldiers arrived in the early 70s to fight the Portuguese.

Any suspicion was soon replaced by great warmth as I was introduced to the neighbours. Bakar, a thin wiry man, was a carpenter. He was relatively well off, having been paid by an aid agency to build houses. Awa, his wife, was a large, bubbly woman with a booming voice. My friend explained who I was. "Nik. Yorrr," she said nodding, eyeing me closely. She asked my friend if I spoke Crioulu. He shook his head and she let out a high-pitched "aahhh" — part disappointment, part understanding. She introduced me to her three daughters who had been waiting shyly behind her. Zora, the eldest, was 16; she smiled and immediately turned away. Fanta and Mima, eight and ten, stared calmly up at me, their angelic faces belied by a sadistic streak that soon emerged.

As we trooped round the back into my friend's house a dreadful wailing started. A heavily pregnant mongrel chained to a wall staggered around a small outhouse. The small girls pulled on the chain dragging the bitch out by her already tight collar. The dog choked and the girls laughed. Its name was Sufre. Very apt, given that Guineans believe it's their fate to suffer impoverishment. A phrase often quoted — *Jito katem* — means 'we have no choice'. Portugal, the colonial master since the 15th century, exploited the country for its groundnuts and palm oil. They made no attempt to understand the culture and customs. A posting here was probably not regarded as a promotion. When they were finally ousted in the early 70s, after Africa's longest independence struggle, it was almost with some relief.

What the Salazar regime left behind was a country whose population was almost totally uneducated, completely dependent on agriculture and with very little infrastructure on which to rebuild itself. Despite the country's lack of interest in Guinea-Bissau, the Portuguese army made a vigorous last stand. Much of the fiercest fighting took place around Catio and a key parting gift was the bombing of the dykes that protected the rice paddies from the sea. It was a spiteful act, and one from which the land here has still not recovered. Sufre continued to howl and I noticed the water bowl just out of her reach.

Awa immediately took it upon herself to start teaching me Crioulu. Lesson one: greetings.

"Nik. *Kuma ti Kurpu* ?" — How is your body? She acted out the words, finally slapping my chest.

"*Stabom, e abo*?" — Well, how is yours?

She laughed and let out a deep husky "Yorrr" of delight.

Greetings were prolonged affairs. Every time you passed someone, particularly an elder, you would ask the same series of questions, starting with a summary of what the person was actually doing at the time.

For example: "Ahh Nik. You are standing." "Yes, I'm standing" "And how is your body?" "My body is good, how is your body?" "My body is well. How is your family?" And then enquiries into the health and well being of family and livestock. In London there is traffic congestion. In Catio there are greetings. Just walking a short distance could take a very long time.

That night we ate by candlelight, the Russian engines having decided to give up for the evening. The fan stopped and the room quietly began to warm. Awa cooked a chicken stew, virulent red from the palm oil, and a leafy vegetable called *baguidje* that fizzed on the tongue. We ate from a huge enamel bowl of rice. A pit was made in the centre, the chicken poured in and then oily, spicy handfuls scooped from bowl to mouth. Rice is the main staple. Before the dry season starts, farmers try and make two harvests. Whatever surplus they have is stored, sold or used to pay their workers. By the end of the dry season many people are eating just rice — sometimes their seed grain. And yet it's in the nature of Guineans to be friendly and generous. If anyone said "*Bin no comi*" — 'come and eat' — I was to rub my stomach and say "*No, me adjuta*" — 'I am full.' If I didn't, I would be expected to share that person's food, no matter how little they had.

On his way to bed my friend casually remarked, "Watch out for Old Seven Legs." I froze. Seven was one short of eight, and eight legs meant spiders. I had come across a particularly large specimen in the capital, Bissau, where I'd almost head-butted it coming though the bathroom curtain. A seven-legged spider could only mean one thing; bitterness, frustration, anger. It would surely take its revenge out on me. My candle was starting to flicker and fade, a small circle of sepia gradually fading to black. I had to hurry if I was to make my bed secure. I placed two chairs wide apart and draped a mosquito net over them, tucking it under the grass mats that made my mattress. Just in time. The candle flickered and died. The floor was hard, the mats pinched and it was 26°C but I was safe, safe from Old Seven Legs, who even now in my mind was growing to gigantic proportions. Bollocks. I heard the familiar high-pitched whine and immediately slapped the side of my head. I also needed to piss. I stared into the dark knowing that I would have to move. It was going to be a long night.

I awoke on May Day to find half my face burning from a string of mosquito bites. Seven Legs was lurking in the bathroom, squeezed between a clay pot and a bar of soap. Outside I could hear laughter and shouting followed by a banging on the door. Two men, both in their early 20s, stood clapping their hands. "Come, come. Let's go."

This was my introduction to Nuno and Cerifo. Nuno was the town's comedian and Cerifo, its casanova, was currently romancing an American Peace Corps worker. Both wore trainers, baseball caps and jeans (only small boys and foreigners wore shorts). The traditional way to spend May Day was to head off for the pristine sandy beaches at Caiar and we would have to hurry to get a seat on the boat. They led the way, carrying bundles of provisions on their heads — rice, palm oil, chillies, bowls and pots. I was struck by their physiques. In fact, nearly all the young men had astonishing bodies. A combination of back-breaking work in the paddy fields and rice-based meals meant they were all muscular and well-proportioned. The young women were equally striking; tall with delicate features that, combined with the fashion for wearing their hair in long, thin plaits, gave them the impression of being a race of beautiful Amazons. *Vogue* would do well to send modelling scouts to Guinea-Bissau. It all served to reinforce just how different I was.

On the way through the outskirts of town, more and more people joined us. We made an odd looking procession — brancos and *bretos*, men, women, pigs on strings and boys with ghetto blasters. There was a lull in the excitement for several hours while a search party went looking for the boat's owner who was still drunk from the night before. It was late afternoon by the time we finally moved off. More than 30 people in a large dinghy with definitely no sign of any life jackets. The cashew wine flowed and the skipper gave up telling people to sit down as he negotiated the narrow avenues of murky water lined with mangrove. Nervous-looking guinea fowl shivered under the seats.

It was dark when we arrived and despite a long walk to the beach, the party continued right into the sea. The water was warm and soon full of bodies splashing and screaming in the moonlight. Sitting in the shallows and feeling the warm breeze waft around me I felt an urge to be naked. Was this my primitive side emerging, I wondered, or just a kinky desire to feel the sea flow around my genitals? I slid my shorts down. A perfect, cloudless night revealed a myriad different stars and constellations. I found the Plough and then Orion's Belt. I sighed; my world was in order. The moment was so perfect that at first the pain didn't register. There it was again, short, stabbing pains. There was something in the water and I wasn't the only one to notice. The tone of the screaming voices changed. Soon everyone was yelping and slapping themselves. Jellyfish. They were everywhere. Each new wave brought a fresh attack. It was time to leave the primitive world. En masse we kicked and splashed our way on to the beach and collapsed on our groundsheet, laughing. Nuno and Cerifo produced a plastic bottle.

"Wiiine, Nik," they sniggered, "Cashew wine," and then handed me the bottle. According to Guineans, brancos can't drink cashew wine. It has the same smell as a freshly ironed sweaty nylon shirt. I slowly poured some into my mouth. It was warm and I could feel soft jelly-like particles flow past my lips. The taste was little more than sugary water but with a dry aftertaste that sucked the moisture from my tongue. It wasn't unpleasant and, as far as I could taste, not the least bit alcoholic. I smacked my lips and let out an exaggerated "aaaahh". They hooted with laughter and clicked their fingers. "You like?" said Cerifo grinning.

"I like too much," I said grabbing the bottle and taking another swig. They both screamed and rocked around helplessly. I had obviously passed an important test.

We spent two nights at Caiar. More boats arrived the next day until more than 100 people were now living, eating and sleeping out in the open. The beach was turned into a strip of football pitches, the sea into a volleyball court. People lounged, drank and drummed. Occasionally men and women would pair up and disappear over the dunes. We had created a new community. But even though I was here and part of it, there were reminders of just how different we really all were. I watched a man preparing his dinner. He held a hen upside down between his knees and, producing a knife, bent over it and sawed into its throat. All the while he talked to a friend. The bird struggled but his grip was strong and soon a small pool of blood formed at his feet, slowly seeping into the sand. He dropped the limp body on the ground and wiped the blade on his T-shirt. I remembered the pigs we brought from Catio. I hadn't seen them for a while.

This life and death theme continued on my return to Catio. I had been introduced to Pedro, an agriculturist working for the government. He was keen to show me how people used the ancient technique of slash and burn to prepare land for cultivation. I had watched amazed as a woman worked an area of bush the size of a football pitch, painstakingly hauling charred branches and stumps to one side. He explained that this was her land, not her husband's, and anything grown on it belonged to her not him.

It was pitch black as we returned to Catio and we drove fast along the empty metalled road. Suddenly I spotted two tiny flashing green lights on the verge ahead of us. Eyes. A large spotted feline bolted out across the road. Then, tragically, as soon as it reached the safety of the other side it leapt back in front of us. We hit it. Pedro stamped on the breaks and we leapt out of the cab, cautiously making our way back, stopping a few feet away from it.

"Onca," said Pedro. "Very rare."

From head to tail it was one and a half metres with a beautiful spotted coat like a cheetah. "Perhaps it's just stunned."

From where I stood it looked like it was smirking. Pedro gingerly kicked its tail. No reaction. He kicked again. Nothing. It was dead. We loaded it into the back of the truck and returned home.

Awa was delighted. She would share it with Pedro. Bakar immediately got to work skinning it. Mima and Fanta squatted around it stroking the fur. Brilliant, I thought. The only wild animal I'd seen in Africa and we'd killed it. What's more I would be eating it tomorrow.

Almost immediately death struck again. This time it was definitely my fault. I had spotted Old Seven Legs in the process of traversing the wire mesh on the door. I was following his progress by torchlight with disgusted fascination when Bakar walked past with the dead cat's coat. He opened the door, and noticing what I was doing tutted, removed one sandal, flipped Seven Legs onto the floor and gave him a good pasting. I can't say

I was too sorry to see him go, but I was beginning to feel like some sort of wildlife jinx.

Death continued to stalk me the next day. I had gone for a bicycle ride in the bush when I heard the sound of drumming. I followed, but every time I reached the end of one path the sound would drift and change direction. I was being drawn deeper into the bush with no real idea of where I was going. Eventually I came to a large clearing. On one side was a compound of low thatched mud huts built in typical Balante style, from which I could hear singing as well as drumming. I dismounted and made my way over. A boy came out to meet me and, by grabbing the bicycle, made me follow him along the side of the huts and into the compound.

The first thing I noticed was a cow lying on the ground, neck slashed and with its head pulled back to reveal the gaping wound. Then I saw the men dancing and a large group of women sitting clapping their hands. A young man dressed in a pearl white robe fringed with turquoise paisley patterns came across to greet me.

His name was Eugenio, a student in Catio, and it was his pleasure to welcome me to the funeral of his father. Unknowingly I had answered the message being played out on the two huge hollowed-out logs or *bombalons*. The dead man was well respected, but this was a joyous occasion since he'd lived a full life and fathered many children. Three cows had been slaughtered in his honour. Eugenio beckoned me to sit next to him and handed me a plastic beaker of cashew wine, its rim so thoroughly chewed it now resembled fur. I sat absorbed in the spectacle. These people had no idea who I was and neither did they care. They were simply carrying out an age-old ritual, one that very few non-Africans would ever encounter. Eugenio had spotted my camera and asked me to take a photo of his family. Bizarrely, he sat them on one of the dead cows. When he asked why I hadn't brought a video camera I was shocked. Every time I thought I was seeing something authentic it was undermined by creeping westernisation.

It was my last night in Catio and we were watching the young men practise their dancing routines for a competition against a neighbouring village. A large crowd had gathered to sing and keep the rhythm. The dancers, about 20 of them, slowly started to jog around in a big circle. On particular beats they stamped their bare feet hard on the ground. The songs grew louder, the rhythms faster and more complicated. The ground trembled as they stamped down harder and harder, their sweating faces lit up by two bonfires. This wasn't a performance put on for tourists, it was just one event in the life of this small town in a country no one cared about. But once again, my image of traditional Africa was confounded. Some of the dancers had Coke cans tied around their ankles as a musical accompaniment to their stamping. This branco Westerner was no longer surprised when he later found himself attempting hip-hop manoeuvres in the nightclub with the very same dancers.

It was time to leave Catio. This time I would be travelling by *kadonga* — a bus journey that would make the truck seem luxurious. Animals and baggage on top, humans inside. But after half an hour it was hard to say who had the better deal. Some things wouldn't be changing for a long time. Africa isn't a theme park for visitors, but traditions will only survive if people want them to — at least in Catio they were still going strong despite any external influences. I smiled, reflecting on Nuno's and Cerifo's parting request: to send them a pair of trainers. Preferably Nike.

A Fulani party on the Niger

by Chris Caldicott

The day began with turbaned Fulani riders galloping out of the Saharan haze on camels and horses, their robes billowing behind them. Arriving at the far bank of the river in clouds of dust, they halted briefly before driving their steeds into the water. Behind them, thousands of head of long-horned cattle thundered toward the bank. This alone made up for the hardships of the journey to reach this remote location for one of Africa's most spectacular migrations. On our side of the river the huge crowd of expectant spectators were nearing a peak of excitement. Their husbands, fathers, sons and brothers were returning after months away in the harsh lands of the northern Sahel, and they were bringing the wealth of the tribe with them. Women in their finest off-the-shoulder dresses made high-pitched rhythmic warbling sounds with their tongues, young men kept up with them on an assortment of drums, and children were hurriedly marshalled away by old men with staffs, to make way for the imminent stampede.

Every year the dry season heat of sub-Saharan Africa turns pastures on the edge of the desert to dust, signalling the time for the semi-nomadic cattle herders of Mali to head south across the Niger river to winter grasslands. Despite the devastating droughts of recent years, this still involves many hundreds of thousands of cattle searching for as safe as possible a point to cross one of Africa's mightiest rivers. As rainfall eases in the tropical mountain rainforests of Guinea at the source of the Niger, the water level drops. Eventually it drops enough to give the Fulani good enough odds to embark on their great exodus.

The usually uneventful village of Diafarabe, built on a narrow strip of land where the Niger meets the Diaka river, is the location of the first and largest of the annual crossings. For a few days this timeless community, living in mud houses without electricity or running water and unconnected to the outside world by anything resembling a road, sees its village transformed into a colourful stage for one of West Africa's most captivating events. With the return of loved ones, it is an emotional gathering of Fulani from all over the region, all of whom have to find a way of travelling to Diafarabe. Despite the inevitable complications, I wanted to join them to witness what promised to be a momentous event. I had also always wanted to go to Timbuktu, a few days' journey further down the Niger from Diafarabe.

When the Niger is full enough, passenger steamers provide a service all the way from the rapids just above Mali's capital Bamako, via Timbuktu to the northern desert outpost of Gao, and pass right by Diafarabe every ten days or so. I travelled to Mali with the intention of taking this steamer journey and including the cattle crossing as a highlight.

Unfortunately the river cannot be deep enough for the steamer to pass, and shallow enough for the cattle to cross at the same time. I needed to find an overland route to Diafarabe and then north to Mopti where, if I was lucky, I could catch the last boat to Timbuktu and on to Gao before that stretch of the Niger also became unnavigable.

As English is rarely spoken in francophone West Africa I was glad of the company of Cécile, a French friend whose West African father had once lived in London. This was Cécile's first trip beyond Europe and she was keen to see a land where she had unexplored roots. I was concerned that Cécile might find travelling in this part of the world too difficult to enjoy. I was quite used to travelling in Africa, but as it turned out, I was the one who was completely unprepared for how hard travel would be in Mali, whereas Cécile took it all in her stride. In Mali the three main ingredients for normal travel — transport, accommodation and food — all became increasingly elusive.

Just getting to Mali had been an adventure. There being no Malian embassy in Britain, we had had to send our passports to Cécile's father in

Paris to get our visas. Then, limited funds had demanded a long-winded route via Moscow, Tripoli and Ouagadougou to Bamako on Aeroflot. Delayed by temperatures of -30°C in Moscow, we watched men with high-pressure steam hoses defrosting our plane, which was packed with Libyan migrant workers returning home. In Tripoli the transit lounge was full of pictures of and books by Gaddafi, but from there the flight gave us stunning, cloudless views of the Sahara.

The first sight of anything other than dramatic mountains and sand dunes was the immensity of the Niger winding its way like a giant snake through the desert. Despite beginning its journey to the sea only 240km inland from the Atlantic coast of Guinea, Africa's third longest river makes a 4,160km arc, reaching right up into the Sahel before turning south again to spill into the Atlantic as a massive delta.

At Bamako every other passenger was met by a posse of excited relatives eager to whisk them away; and within a few minutes of landing the airport was empty and being locked up, the staff having piled into their cars and left too. We had to walk to the main road and wait for a bus into town.

The combination of heat, jet lag and culture shock gave us an excuse to spend our first night at the budget-crippling Grand Hotel where we slept in air-conditioned, colonial luxury. Aware of the need to find somewhere more affordable to spend the rest of our time in Bamako, we set off in the relative cool of the morning to explore the options. These consisted of an iron bed in the very shabby mosquito-infested dormitory of a Catholic convent where the nuns operated a 10pm curfew, or for five times the price, a sleazy windowless room in a noisy brothel. We went to a café for lunch and a think.

The café staff said we were welcome to sleep on their tables after closing time if we were desperate. We were. Fortunately this worked out well: the café was a social hub for Bamako's musicians, some of whom would play live here during the evenings. We soon grew fond of Bamako, but our stay was limited by the need to leave plenty of time for the uncertain journey to Diafarabe.

The first stage of the journey from Bamako to Segou was relatively straightforward, squeezed into a battered Peugot 504 bush-taxi, speeding north. Segou was an easy place to spend a few days negotiating our onward passage. To travel beyond Segou without one's own vehicle requires patience and luck. There is a dirt track as far as Ke Macina, and from there to Diafarabe there were only vague rumours of passable terrain.

As the day of the crossing approached, demand among the Fulani for space on the Diafarabe-bound vehicles increased. Mindful of this, the owners of trucks were biding their time in expectation of premium fares. The French owner of the hotel where we stayed helped us find a man with a truck who agreed to take us. We spent our days waiting, eating wonderful peppery groundnut stews and barbecued brochettes of river perch fresh from the Niger. We took long walks along the banks of the river by day and spent memorable evenings in moonlit courtyards listening to excellent local musicians.

We arrived at the truck well before our dawn departure, eager for an early getaway. It was getting dark again, however, before our truck owner was satisfied that the number of people crammed in the back had reached a threshold of discomfort that not even his greed could exceed. We drove a few hundred metres and stopped. Everyone had to get out and pay their fares in advance so the driver could buy petrol. This became a voluble and animated negotiation. When at last petrol could be purchased it had to be poured painstakingly by hand from a watering can. The equation of fitting all the passengers back into the truck was complicated and very time-consuming, yet surprisingly good-humoured.

After a few minutes of slow progress into the desert night we came to our first police checkpost. Everybody out. Papers had to be checked. The police were drunk and belligerent. They bullied and pushed people around and found plenty of problems with their papers. It was an ugly scene with little sign of compromise. The driver decided we would sleep the night at the checkpost and start again in the morning.

We woke to find all the male passengers prostrated in morning prayers, a faint glow of dawn in the eastern sky. In 24 hours we had only travelled about three kilometres. The policemen were sleepy and grumpy, but they soon agreed a sum of money with the driver which would allow them to overlook any imagined irregularities with peoples' papers. A quick whip-round among all the passengers accumulated the funds.

For the rest of the day we bumped along in almost intolerable heat and dust and extreme discomfort, relieved by numerous stops for prayers, police, passengers and petrol. Although each stop inevitably added at least an hour to the journey, they always provided a welcome chance to stretch cramped limbs and see a bit of the country we were travelling through. For most of the journey the view was obscured by the metal sides of our airless torture chamber.

Whenever someone got off at a village they would be replaced by more northbound Fulani until everybody in the truck was bonded by a common destination. When a very grand, finely dressed man embarked, he was given the best place sitting in the cab. During the next prayer stop he came over for a chat. In fluent French, he told Cécile he was a Fulani chief and we would be his guests in Diafarabe. His hospitality began with an invitation to Cécile to join him in the comfort of the cab. She tried in vain to decline on the basis she would have to take someone's seat, but the chief would have none of it.

By the time the truck deposited us all, in the middle of nowhere and in darkness, Cécile and the chief were good friends. I was shattered from the conditions in the back, and considerably poorer after the checkpoints.

I didn't mind though; my fellow passengers had been friendly, charming and good-humoured through all the suffering. It was just a shame the money had ended up in the hands of the greedy police. My contributions were about to be well rewarded anyway, by the generosity of the chief. We didn't have a clue where we were. The night was very dark and silent. We followed the others, and as they walked the women began to sing. When we reached water they started yelping as though imitating wild animals. Then they were silent and we all sat down to wait. Out of the darkness some *pirogues* (small wooden boats) were paddled to the shore. We all climbed in. Unseen on the far bank was Diafarabe. Slowly we made out its dark shapes under a million stars.

The chief led us between dried mud buildings and through a maze of narrow alleyways to his compound. The village was completely still, and dramatic silhouettes of mosques and palm trees towered above us. On the chief's roof, sleep came easily as we realised we had just made it — the crossing was due to begin the next morning.

The event lived up to all our expectations. All day wave after wave of cattle crossed the Diaka, raced over the floodplain and up the bank into the narrow streets of the village, then down into the Niger and across it to fresh pastures. The herders shouted, whistled and wielded sticks at their confused livestock. Occasionally a bull would break free and run amok, to the great delight of the crowd. Trying to capture all of this on film became something of a challenge at times; not only was there stampeding livestock, there were also clouds of dust and crushes of people.

At nightfall there was music and dancing. A tractor-battery-powered megaphone was hooked up to a flute. The flautist played with such ability, speed and feedback, that the effect was like a heavy rock guitar solo. He was backed by manic drummers performing with equal volume and energy. By contrast the dancing was tame at first, just some teenage girls shuffling about with their backs to the crowd. As the pace of the music picked up, however, older women joined in. With sudden bursts of energy they sprang their bodies up and whipped their torsos through the air, arms waving until they were leaning over backwards.

Bumping into some of our fellow passengers from the journey inevitably meant their insistence on supplying us with food and drink like old friends. After a couple of days of this we were keen to move on, though. Getting away from Diafarabe proved no easier than getting there. We still wanted to try and get to Mopti in time to catch the last steamer of the season to Timbuktu. The few Mopti-bound motorised pirogues were full to an absurdly dangerous point before we could even get close enough to attempt negotiating a passage. Our hosts advised us to try and get to the closer town of Djenne in time for the weekly Monday market after which there would be plenty of pirogues heading back to Mopti.

The road to Djenne was as slow and nonexistent as the one between Ke Macina and Diafarabe. Djenne is a 15th century settlement of the same vintage as Timbuktu, yet much better preserved and more lively. The Sudanese mud architecture — of the massive sandcastle mosque and the merchants' houses connected by a labyrinth of winding alleyways — is the finest in the Sahel. The market in front of the mosque saw tribal people gather from the surrounding countryside. Dressed in their finest, they were considerably more spectacular than the dried vegetables they were selling.

As promised, we found an afternoon pirogue for Mopti. Some Nigerian men on board, heading up to Gao to hitch a ride across the Sahara to Libya in search of jobs, gave me my first opportunity in days to speak in English to anyone except Cécile. We were still wide awake and chatting at 3am when we saw the first electric lights of the journey. The boulevard waterfront of Mopti looked like an elegant, even romantic, cosmopolitan river port, quite deserted but full of promise.

Dawn proved this to be mostly an illusion. We had all slept on the boat next to Le Bozo café. The Bozo are a tribe of fishermen, the café is next to their market, and we woke to find ourselves in the middle of a very busy, loud and chaotic scene. It was short on romance and elegance, but big on the smell of fish heating up in the fierce morning sun. Opting against the odours, I choose to spend a couple of days trekking in nearby Dogon country.

The Dogon people, worshippers of the Dog Star Sirius, live in hamlets of tiny flat-roofed mud houses surrounded by conical straw-roofed granaries, all built improbably into or around the spectacular 300m cliff of the rocky Bandiagara Escarpment. A sheer drop runs for more than 320km separating two levels of the Sahel which are only connected by a network of paths and steep climbs. It has protected this eccentric area, and it has hardly been penetrated by Islam. It is a much older Africa, like something from a Tolkien fantasy. It is also very hot and rugged. I squeezed into a battered jeep for a bumpy ride to Bankass on the edge of Dogon Land. There I met up with a German doctor and his Chinese wife who invited me to join them and their guide for a couple of days' walking to the villages of Ende and Kanicombole at the base of the escarpment and then on to Djiguibombo high above it.

Taking a guide is often a mixed blessing. As well as being helpful in finding the right paths, in Dogon Land it is compulsory for visits to some villages, including Kanicombole, and useful for negotiating somewhere to sleep and eat without falling foul of traditional courtesies. On the other hand, guides can be expensive, troublesome and annoying. Amadou was a mixed blessing. Bankass is full of would-be guides, some are genuinely Dogon and probably worth the high fee they ask, others are youth from other tribes who spend most of their time sitting around under trees, smoking cigarettes and trying to pick up some of the lucrative work. Amadou was from Mopti and did know his way around, but spoke little Dogon, and was more prone to arguing than negotiating, both with us and the Dogon.

Things started off well enough. At Ende, Amadou introduced us to the *dugu-tigi* (village headman), who gave us some space to sleep on a flat roof, and some bowls of millet, rice and sauce. He then disappeared. Ende is built right under an immense overhang of the escarpment, and I found sleeping with several thousand tons of solid rock suspended above my heads was very eerie. The Dogon ignored us completely, probably because Amadou had upset them over how much they would receive for putting us up. Their ideas about cameras stealing their souls makes it impolite to photograph them, but the village and landscape are spectacularly photogenic. I spent the dusty orange hours of dusk busy with my camera.

Next morning there was no sign of Amadou. When he eventually turned up just before midday we had had enough of being ignored in Ende, the sun was at its hottest, and he was demanding more money to take us on to Kanicombole. As he had hardly done anything yet we protested. Amadou flew into a violent rage, accusing us of being rich exploitative foreigners while he was just a poor African. He even threatened to set the Dogon on us, hinting that the only reason we hadn't been murdered in our beds was due to his protection. Amadou stormed off to have an equally heated altercation with the dugu-tigi, who like all the other villagers showed no intention of doing anything other than continuing to ignore us.

Despite the rules about guides and the almost unbearable heat, we decided to make our own way to Kanicombole. At a point where exhaustion and thirst were close to defeating us, Amadou appeared as if nothing had happened, announced it was his birthday, and presented each of us with a bottle of Coke. He also had plenty of drinking water. In Kanicombole he found us another roof, some more millet, rice and sauce and vanished.

Next morning he was back at dawn to lead us up to Djiguibombo, after another row with the villagers. The climb up the escarpment was the highlight of the trek and Djiguibombo as compelling as the other villages. But after two days of heat and Amadou, I was exhausted.

Cécile, by contrast, was relaxed and ready to board the *Timbouctou* which had just docked at the Mopti jetty. Our second class tickets entitled us to a decidedly grim, cramped and airless cabin, which we had to share with a Fulani village chief and his considerable entourage of sycophantic hangers-on. Although only he and one of his wives at a time were supposed to use the other two beds, there were often up to seven people in the tiny cabin during the day. The chief had bagged the two bottom bunks, and at night he spread his massive bulk on one and his possessions on the other, leaving his gang to sleep on deck.

We never saw him leave the cabin during the ten-day voyage, and although he was always impeccably polite to us, it was very clear he appreciated our daily absence from the cabin. This was no hardship as the cabin was as hot as hell and smelt like a bordello. After the first uncomfortable sleepless night I even gave up sleeping in there. At 5am the chief noisily washed his feet in the tiny hand basin between the bunks, then invited all the men in his party to do the same, before they started the long ritual of prostration and prayer.

The price of our tickets also included some equally grim food. Having witnessed the crew washing our lettuce in a mixture of brown river water and bleach we decided to solve both situations by sleeping on the first class deck and buying our meals from families down in third class. Cooking extra food and selling it to subsidise the third class fare seemed to be a well-established operation on the lower deck and we were spoilt for choice. My mouth still waters at the thought of sweet potatoes cooked with lots of fresh ginger, garlic and cayenne pepper in a creamy peanut butter sauce, served with fried plantains and homemade ginger beer.

In the evenings we hung out in the first class bar where the only drink on sale was *pastis* and the only other customer, a Frenchman who was renting one of the two first class cabins. The other was occupied by yet another Malian chief and his entourage.

Etienne had come to Mali to visit his sister who was married to a diplomat at the French embassy. These connections were very handy at unfriendly police roadblocks when we shared a journey back to Bamako with him at the end of our river trip.

At times the Niger carves an improbable passage through cliffs of golden sand, the desert stretching as far as the eye can see in every direction. Such a long time on an uncomfortable boat could have been tedious, but it never was. We saw hippos in the river and camels on the banks and the boat's arrival was a major event everywhere we stopped. An advance reception committee of little boats, selling firewood, fish, vegetables, cooking oil and fresh fruit would be followed by a siege of sellers as soon as we came within wading distance of a village. Nearing the boat's namesake, negotiating the narrow channels of the island delta and winding around the shallows, it became obvious why this was the last sailing of the year.

The Niger has changed course away from Timbuktu. Once a centre of Islamic scholarship and a mighty empire, today it is something of a lifeless backwater. From its humble beginnings as a Tuareg settlement about 1,000 years ago, Timbuktu grew to be a flourishing terminal of Saharan caravan routes. Merchants from Djenne and Walata moved and set up business, much to the resentment of the original Tuareg inhabitants. This resentment turned violent. In response to pleas from merchants, the 14th century King of Mali, Mansa Musa, took control, bringing fabulous wealth with him. Timbuktu's reputation as a city of riches began to spread. As the 15th century Songhai empire of the Sudanese king Sunni Ali became the most powerful in the Sahara, Timbuktu became a thriving western outpost of Songhai wealth.

The following century saw Sudanese power in the region replaced by that of Morocco, and the caravan route from Timbuktu to Zagora and Marrakesh became one of the busiest across the Sahara. Through the centuries the Tuareg kept their distance as nomads in the desert, but they never forgot their designs on Timbuktu. At any time of weakness they preyed mercilessly on the caravans, and even robbed the merchants on the city streets. Rumours of Timbuktu's fabled wealth lived on long after intimidation from the Tuareg had sent the city into permanent decline. By the time 19th century explorers from northern Europe risked life and limb to be the first of their kind to visit the city, Timbuktu was already a rather sad shadow of its former glory. The downward spiral has never been reversed. Now Timbuktu attracts travellers because of its name rather than any great riches.

Gao, another two days downriver, had much more of the atmosphere of a bustling desert outpost. This really is the last place before the largest desert on the planet. There is a frontier-town mentality in the bar of the Hotel Atlantide. Travellers arriving from the north are high on relief and celebrating their safe arrival, while those coming from the south drown their anxieties in a last night of excess before the uncertainties of the journey ahead. Among the tombs, mosques and markets there are Tuareg men in desert robes, veiled by scarves of vivid blue and green. Women are not just unveiled, but full of flirtatious confidence. Despite being as far as I have ever felt from everything I know, at the most distant point of a long journey, I was unexpectedly made to feel close to home when I came across a plinth marking the Greenwich Meridian Line. After all it had taken to reach here, it was just a straight line from here all the way to London.

Swazi religion and quasi-religion

by Sharon Harris

"You don't mind me wearing traditional costume?" asked Mandla before we, six independently travelling female backpackers, embarked on our 'Swaziland on a Sunday' experience. Mandla began by telling us that our church visit was going to be his first in about a year, so we naturally assumed his attire was his Sunday best. Until, that is, he added, "They're Manzini Wanderers' colours." The day was destined to be full of religious experiences. A normal Sunday in Swaziland — church in the morning followed by a soccer match in the afternoon. The old religion and the new religion in perfect harmony.

The service was to be held in the royal village of Lobamba, originally built in 1830 for King Sobhuza I before becoming Sobhuza II's royal *kraal*. First we had to get there, and in Swaziland if you don't have your own transport this means hitching a lift with someone who does own wheels of some description. All thoughts of safety standards go out the window — as would the majority of the vehicle's occupants if the vehicle was suddenly and abruptly brought to a halt. Quite how seven people were going to find a car with seven spare seats was unimaginable, but that particular transportation difficulty was soon overcome with the miraculous arrival of a minibus taxi, of sorts. Our prayers were already being answered. What we didn't know was that in Africa there is no such thing as a space when it comes to cramming people into a vehicle or anything else people have to fit in to. Intimacy with your fellow passengers develops quite easily; the difficulty lies in extricating the fare from your pocket when someone is sat on your hand or lap. We discreetly attempted to gather together two rand each so that when the moment of payment arose we would be prepared. When it did arrive nobody had the slightest inkling as to who was or wasn't paying. The coins made their way to the front and the man with a bag seemed quite happy that the correct amount of coins had been forwarded to him.

As we travelled to Lobamba Mandla briefed us in Swazi culture and history. Swazi monarchs are always men from the Dlamini family. During his reign the king marries a number of women from different clans. By marrying in this way it is claimed that national unity is promoted and upheld. As the king notches up marriages it is held that the last wife has come from a more important family member than the last. In theory this means that the son of the very last wife should be the heir to the throne, but the reality is that all the older sons have their sights set on becoming king. When the king dies he leaves a nation with power struggles.

Following the king's demise, the *liquqo* (royal council) selects the queen mother who rules as regent until her son is capable of taking control. King Sobhuza II died in 1982 and the Queen Mother Dzeliwe assumed the regency. She was deposed by Prince Bhekimpi who ruled until 1985, eliminating any opposition he could find, though only until the current king returned to Swaziland from the UK.

It soon became clear that the population of less than one million is intensely loyal to the monarchy. From the window we could see women wearing red sarongs with the face of the King emblazoned on the cloth. King Mswati III, educated in Britain, succeeded to the throne in 1986 and, at the age of 32, has been rather restrained and only taken seven wives to date (his father King Sobhuza had 70 women).

"Is that one for each day of the week?" I jested. "Monday, Tuesday, Wednesday…" before biting my lip. I'd remembered hearing about the Nyonyane (Little Bird) Mountain or, as it was known to early settlers, Execution Hill — a rather formidable mountain from which people found guilty of treason were, in times past, hurled to certain death. I wasn't going down that road or indeed over that edge.

I was intrigued to learn the King already had 13 children while I, a mere three years younger, had none. The king's opportunity to select a wife takes place in late August or early September each year. The *Umhlanga* is a fertility dance which gets its name from the reeds gathered by young women and taken to the queen mother's residence to repair her kraal. On the sixth and seventh days, the women clothed in elaborate and carefully coded costumes dance and sing in front of the Queen Mother and the King in the hope he will choose one of them as a new bride.

Soon we arrived in the village of Lobamba and piled out of the van onto the dusty roadside, a major feat in itself considering our positions at the back. People don't move out and get back in afterwards, so you just climb over them. Strangely, they didn't seem to mind being trodden on. I suppose they're used to their transport system and its peculiarities.

We ambled through the village and stopped at Mandla's house, which he shared with his mother, siblings, assorted youngsters, cats and chickens. His mother, under strict instruction not to tidy for visitors, was busy working in the kitchen. This is a woman's job, although in Africa it seems that aside from lounging around and brewing and consuming beer, every job is a woman's job. In general, the women in Africa are nothing short of amazing. They think absolutely nothing of walking miles with one baby strapped to their back, one on their front, a huge bag of Mealie Meal balanced on their head and bags in each hand. And they don't complain. African women, far from being the underclass, are really the driving force behind the African way of life. They are an inspiration. Mandla's mother had been rather progressive. His father had treated her badly, so in a Catholic society where divorce isn't a consideration, she walked away and made a new life for herself and her children. Mandla said we would return after church, but we had to hurry because the service was due to start. We arrived at St Mary's Church slightly after 10.30am and the choir already seemed in full vocal flow. What were the other villagers going to make of us all? We stood out somewhat. Mandla, on the other hand, was making a rare religious visit and was choosing to do so in the company of six Western females. We couldn't resist pulling his leg.

"We're your new wives," we joked to the poor lad who was adamant that he would never marry. "You nearly have as many wives as King Mswati III," we continued. At 29 he already had two children and was happy with that. A wife would be too much of a complication in his life…

or so he thought and so he told us. Singing was already in progress so we slipped in at the back of the airy building and found ourselves a pew. Here, again, there was no such thing as a space, and people crammed themselves in. The side opposite was more spacious; reed mats designed for mothers and small children to sit and stand upon. Comfortable they were not, but practical they were. One little girl, sporting a blue denim pinafore, was having none of the sitting down lark and danced merrily in the aisle throughout the service... all two-and-a-half hours of it.

The service was conducted in Siswati, the native language, with occasional interjections in English. We gathered that this was intended for us. Any doubts on this score were soon dismissed when the priest welcomed the "English and German guests" and prayed for us and our families. Particularly moving was the faith they had in us. We were from foreign lands and it was assumed that six Western females had the power to change things for the better, or at least had a better chance of doing so than they did. They prayed for us so that we could change the world. A lump appeared in my throat and I tried not to cry. We mimed to the hymns and threw in the odd "Alleluia" when we'd worked out the pattern. Behind me a man thought I could do with some assistance and continually whispered instructions to me.

"Sit down," "kneel," "stand up." I felt as though I was undergoing puppy training in a dog obedience class. He's being helpful, I assured myself, not exerting dominance. We joined the masses traipsing up the aisle to place emalangeni or rand onto the collection plate and then returned to our seats, not entirely sure as to whether we had been generous enough with our offerings.

The church was doing well as people gave liberally even though, judging from the rustic conditions in the mud hut village, they had very little. But they gave of their own free will, their religion being a central pivot in their everyday lives. Their lives may be basic by Western standards, but they are happy.

Giving didn't stop there. The singing started again and two lines of women slowly shimmied, swayed and jiggled in time to the music. They danced in procession towards the priest, laden with apples, bags of fruit and basic food.

Until Mandla informed me that they were gifts for the priest to live on for the week, I had been rather bemused by the offerings. I hoped he liked oranges because there was a large bag of them being carried on the shoulders of a rather rotund, jolly looking woman.

"Is it always the same women every week?" I enquired.

"No," replied Mandla. "You can go up if you have a gift to give," he said, looking expectantly at my camera. I had other ideas and was thinking more along the lines of the free pair of British Airways socks that I'd acquired on my flight to South Africa. The fact that the priest had known we were going to attend was re-enforced when he said that he'd like the English and German guests to evaluate the music. He hoped it would be good and up to the standards we would expect because, after all, Germany was the birthplace of music. Completely uncultured, I assumed he was referring to the Beatles playing Hamburg and was a very with-it priest to know about Western popular music. It turned out he'd meant Beethoven.

After the service we were greeted by the priest and some of the congregation who were anxious to meet the visitors. Mandla urged him not to alter the service for the benefit of future foreign guests. The priest had other ideas, and was revelling in the new additions to his congregation. He wanted the foreigners to be able to understand his sermons even if it was at the expense of the general flock. It would be his weekly moment of glory. He was only being human. As this conversation went on some of the girls asked to visit the ladies. They returned from the nuns' quarters very excited at the discovery of the stark contrast between the facilities there and in the village.

"The nuns have stereos and videos," they reported. The message was clear. Join the sisterhood for a better way of life. When God calls, technology arrives. Mandla decided that the social chit-chat had to end if we were to get to the football on time. He chatted to friends enroute while we walked along the dusty track, surveying the rubbish strewn around the area and contemplating the fact that the living quarters of those serving God were vastly superior to anything found in the village. Did the people know? If so, did they mind?

We returned to Mandla's place for some pumpkin porridge before the game. The children shyly watched us, remaining mute as we tried to communicate with them in a motherly fashion. We sprawled on some reed mats, dipping our spoons into Mandla's plate, and played with their Western, white, dolls. The task of dressing the toys was made that much easier by remarkable displays of ingenuity. The children would amputate the odd plastic head, leg or arm, then fit the item of clothing and click the missing limb back into place. If only mothers the world over could apply a similar technique, then preparing a child for school in the morning would be so much easier.

We rushed to what was going to be our second religious experience of the day — the soccer match. This was, apparently, a big game and the home supporters were out in force. Manzini Wanderers versus Mbabane Highlanders in the Somhlolo stadium — the country's major sporting and entertainment venue.

Walking to the stadium I asked Mandla what his name meant. I told him mine, Sharon, was found in the Song of Solomon and it meant a plain, a flat area of land. There was a rose of Sharon. He knew the biblical reference and told me he liked names that had meanings. I chose not to tell him that my parents had named me after the female character in *The Champions* — a cult British television series of the late 60s in which three superhumans fought to maintain world peace. His moniker meant 'Lord's power' and he told me he got his name because he failed to cry at birth. They hit him with a ruler and prayed to God and he began to breathe properly and cry. They believed the Lord's power had enabled him to live and thus the only son in a family full of daughters gained his name.

On our arrival at the stadium we paid the equivalent of 50p and attempted to find a space. Of course, in Swaziland there's no such thing as space. Young children, boys and girls, walked around the stands carrying cardboard boxes containing cans of Coke and Castle beer as well as nuts and other edible treats. Someone in the crowd would beckon them and they'd spend an age trying to calculate the change. Men in Manchester United and Liverpool FC shirts stood peacefully side by side and plenty of other females in the crowd made us feel less outnumbered. Tottenham Hotspurs and Liverpool FC are the favourite English soccer teams in Swaziland, by virtue of the fact that they've played in the country. Even those that weren't born at the time know about the day in 1958 when Swaziland defeated Tottenham. It's their equivalent of the England 1966 World Cup victory.

As for the match, no one looked remotely like scoring. Unsurprisingly, both teams needed to create more space. Fans watched the action with radios perched on their shoulders, the volume at full blast. The commentator, for we could all hear him in a more plural form of stereo, tried to inject a feel of drama into the proceedings. The alternative was to gaze ahead at the mountains and the ever-changing shapes of the shadows.

Half-time entertainment emerged in the form of an ingenious acrobatic and magic display that was far more enthralling than the goalless second half. Three athletic men balanced on shoulders and heads and performed feats of levitation. Spontaneous rounds of applause echoed through the stadium. During the performance, four- and five-digit numbers resounded over the tannoy and we eventually twigged that the numbers on our entry tickets were doubling as raffle ticket numbers.

Extra time needed to be played before the match would go to penalties and guarantee some excitement. Totally against the run of play, Mbabane Highlanders scored in the second half of extra time. The exodus began. I didn't want to go. None of us wanted to leave. Didn't anyone remember what happened when Manchester United played Bayern Munich in the final of the European Cup? Manchester United equalised in the final minute and scored again in injury time to seize the cup from the grasp of the German team.

Our reason for leaving was simple. It wasn't that we'd lost faith in our team, it was more to do with the fact that we had to find a bus to squeeze onto. The terraces had begun to empty — and it seemed the same could be said of the beer cans being brandished by the supporters who'd already given up on their team. Judging by their raucous ramblings, the beer had gone down well. As we legged it out of the stadium, dodging scarf-waving fans, the final whistle sounded. Manzini Wanderers had lost one-nil. There were to be no Manchester United-type miracles for them.

Having victoriously fought for seats at the rear of the coach, we uttered a silent prayer for a safe journey home. We didn't want a trip to heaven or hell as the third religious experience of the day. Once the seats were fully occupied the aisles began to fill to bursting point. I stared out of the window half-expecting a representative from the *Guinness Book of World Records* to be standing outside dutifully counting the number of people entering the vehicle. Swazis hung onto the racks, the ceiling, each other or whatever they could cling on to as they squashed closer and closer together. Pairs of eyes stared at us through an assortment of limbs. We, the foreign females, were doing something completely alien — sitting one person to a seat. It wasn't hard to read the minds behind those beady eyes. They were showing full signs of an inner turmoil. Would they try and sit on our laps or respect this strange cultural concept of 'space' that we were blatantly exhibiting?

In the end they allowed us our space, and when the coach could take no more bodies, we lurched out of the car park and into the darkness of the night. It then dawned on us that somehow we were going to have to exit this vehicle wherever and whenever our stop arrived. This same trick had not been that easy earlier on in the day in a much smaller bus. Now was not the time to lose sight of Mandla. He would know where and when, but the process of negotiating the aisle was going to be a whole new ball game.

"Now," he instructed. We rose from our seats and decided on our tactics. Any hopes of a straightforward push-past were soon dashed, and an assault course technique was soon employed. Down on the floor, crawling through legs, around the edges of seats, climbing over the seats.

"Where are you from?" they asked as we endeavoured to force our way to the front before the bus stopped and then decided to take off again.

"The UK, Manchester United, Liverpool... Sorry, was that your leg I just stepped on?" No one seemed to mind and we soon ceased apologising. They were all familiar with the exit procedure. One by one we popped out of the door like corks being prised from champagne bottles. Somewhere outside was a patch of ground, but all we could do was leap into oblivion and hope to employ a parachute-jump-style landing if the need arose.

We walked a further ten minutes along a dark road, trying to keep to the side just in case some vehicle decided to career off the road. After the revelry of the soccer match it was an entirely probable scenario. Next to our hostel stood a bar-cum-restaurant-cum-pick-up joint where women were seeking trade; the only market open on a Sunday night.

Monday dawned, meaning the more respectable markets were going to have to be explored for all their African crafts and assorted wares. We had our own minibus to transport us, but after the previous day's local transport adventures it felt anti-climactic. By Swazi standards there was too much room available and the feeling was that we should be stopping and letting people clamber in. A 12km journey brought us to Swaziland's largest town — Manzini — where we were to do the stereotypical girl thing — shopping. The large market probably sells every conceivable bit of tat anyone could ever wish for — fake designer goods, foodstuffs, and household items included. The upper level contained wooden crafts, paintings, stone sculptures and batiks from a whole range of African countries. To the untrained eye it is impossible to tell, so in order to be sure, it's always best to ask.

"Is that from Swaziland? No. Mozambique, eh?" The only sure thing was that the goods were cheap and came with the reputation of being the best value in the country. If you wanted to make a purchase, best do it here. Haggling was pretty much expected and offers were in abundant supply.

"Buy one wooden mask for seven rand fifty or two for ten." The sellers were doing a fair trade, if not exactly roaring. The lower level contained the fabrics section so we weaved our way through a mass of higgledy-piggledy stalls in search of bargains. The girls were in the market for sarongs. We wisely decided to bypass one of the more interesting units – what could only be described as the hairdressing salon. Swazi people sat in full view of the shoppers while having their whiskers trimmed, heads shaved, or a swift cut.

"Do you want your hair cut?" we were asked. A trip to the hairdressers can be a precarious event even in your own country, when you can explain your preferred style in your native language. Trusting our locks to the person wielding scissors in this establishment was not a risk any of us were willing to take. It would be daring to a fatal degree.

Eventually we arrived at a row of stalls selling sarongs. The many women manning the shops were intensely eager to sell us the King Mswati III special and seemed a little surprised that none of us snapped up the items when they displayed them in their full glory. Haggling began, but the women refused to go less than R15. The girls offered R12 and both sides refused to budge.

"I can get that cheaper in Thailand," argued one as though it was just across the way. The stall holders vehemently stuck to their non-negotiable prices. Thailand it would have to be. Across the road from the main market, stalls were selling fruit and vegetables. Interspersed amongst them was the tent-enclosed stand of Mr France Hlamini, who could well have been a *sangoma*, a traditional diviner chosen by the ancestors of a particular family, or an *inyanga*, a pharmaceutical and medical specialist. He seemed to be masquerading as both because, when not talking about his collection of wives and children, he quite revelled in posing for pictures and displaying the solid and liquid substances on sale.

"What's that orange liquid in the Fanta bottle?" someone enquired. France could hardly contain his vagueness in his answer to its curative properties.

"Orangeade," I muttered cynically. "Probably a good medicine for quenching thirst." Shopping might have been close to being our third religious experience, but this required a leap of faith too far.

Battling through the Sudan

by Geoff Crowther

A s the 20th century approached, the scramble for control of Africa was in full swing. In Sudan, the Madhist forces in control of Khartoum and the British, French, Germans and Belgians were vying over who would rule the lower Nile region. Today, in the same steamy, mosquito-infested equatorial forests and swamps of the south, the battle continues. Only now the combatants have changed, and changed radically.

Once regarded as 'impenetrable' by explorers such as Stanley — though he did eventually make it in his bid to rescue Emin Pasha at the head of Lake Albert — roads (of a sort) and even the occasional railway now criss-cross the area. The roads may have arrived, but the war hadn't left. For the last 16 years the bullets and bombs have continued to fly during violent clashes between the forces of the Sudan People's Liberation Army and those of the Khartoum Government. This is basically a religious war: Islam versus Christian/animist, with the main issue being the attempted imposition of Sharia (Islamic Law) on the north by the Khartoum government in the south. Not even the Muslims of the north, though, are unanimous about this.

I first travelled through Sudan some 30 years ago in the days of Colonel el-Nimeiry. I crossed over from Tessenei (then a part of Ethiopia, but now in Eritrea) to Kassala in a refugee bus before travelling across the desert to Khartoum on the top of trucks. From there it was down the Nile by a combination of river steamers and hitching until I reached the southern 'capital' of Juba. In those days you could do that trip in realtive safety and then head east by road for 300km through Torit and Kapoeta before ending up in Lokichokio, northern Kenya, or continue south along the Nile and cross into Uganda via Nimule.

But times had changed. I was curious, though, about just how much they had changed and wanted to know what effect the war had had on this part of Africa. I knew one thing for certain, no overland trucks had taken this route for years.

Anyone who has followed that route through what was then northern Zaire will never forget it. But even that route is now impossible because of the intractable war between Kabila's forces from Kinshasa in the DRC (supported by troops from Zimbabwe, Angola and Namibia), and various scattered rebel groups who are backed by the armies from Uganda and Rwanda. Like most political situations in Africa it is a complicated mess.

With all the old routes cut off, my travelling companion Kevin and I needed to work out how to get into Sudan from the south. We knew the permit treadmill was going to be long and involved but had no idea where to start. Some contacts who had been involved in distributing food aid in the region told us the first stop was the headquarters for the Sudan Relief and Rehabilitation Association in Nairobi's north-eastern suburbs. Predictably there was no signpost to help us find the building, but through a combination of helpful locals and guesswork we managed to find it. After dealing with the bureaucratic red tape about what passports we did or didn't require and questions about our onward travel movements we got our permits. We booked our overnight bus to Kampala, Uganda's capital.

After the disastrous years of Idi Amin's, Obote's and Okello's rule, Kampala hasn't emerged unscathed, but the shot-out windows and looted buildings are now a thing of the past. At one time, after the Asians were thrown out of the country by Amin, it was almost impossible to find a good curry in Uganda. Now there are new places opening all the time and the Hindu temple near the Nakasero market is busier than it has been for decades — a true sign that the worst years are over and that the people are optimistic about the future.

We had plenty of time to relax and soak up the city's urban ambience over a few beers before we booked our bus ticket to Arua, so we went looking for somewhere to have a drink. There are a number of lively bars, and even nightclubs and a casino in Kampala, but we headed for the Sheraton Hotel. It might not have been typical of our regular haunts, but it is at leat the most reliable place to send and receive faxes. There is also the London Bar in the basement. It had been a long time since I'd been in a London pub, but this place brought the memories flooding back. Beer mats, posters and the beer had been imported. We even managed a game or two of darts in the air-conditioned gloom before heading back out into the wall of heat and chaos outside.

In theory the bus was supposed to leave at 5am. Six was a more realistic departure time as the drivers took a while to get themselves organised. Then there was the obligatory 30-minute revving of the engine. Baggage cluttered the aisles and the overhead luggage racks were stuffed with a vaguely useful collection of recycled plastic bottles and jerry cans. Miraculously the seats were numbered. Even more so was the fact that the passengers used them.

Once out of Kampala's traffic crush the bus hurtled north-west for Packwach and the bridge over the White Nile. The bus screamed past army checkpoints and trucks full of exuberant Ugandan soldiers brandishing AK47s and returning from the war in neighbouring Congo.

There was a relative feeling of security in Kampala. It hadn't always been that way. Until recently the rag-bag teenage rebel units of Joseph Kony's Lord's Resistance Army terrorised much of this area, razing villages, trashing crops, shooting everyone in sight and abducting young girls. Fortunately that era seems to have ended and Kony is under house arrest in Sudan in an effort to patch-up relations with Uganda.

After nine hours of dusty roads we sighed with relief as the bus rolled back onto tarmac for the final stretch into Arua. We settled back and made the most of it. From here on we'd be faced with potholed dirt tracks.

Arua is a fairly prosperous town with banks, bars, a post office and reasonable hotels. It even has a disco. After we had grabbed a bite to eat we went down to the *matatu* stand to look for a pick-up or minibus to Koboko, the junction of the borders of Uganda, Congo and Sudan.

Although everything looks chaotic at a Ugandan minibus stand, once you enter the fray it is easy enough to make sense of what is happening. Touts cajoled us as we fought our way through the crowds of people, who seemed to be loaded down with all the possessions and children they owned. The air was filled with the shouts of destinations, punctuated by the slapping of the bodywork — all in the drive to attract passengers.

We found the stand and were virtually manhandled into the back of the matatu. To the untrained eye it looked almost ready to depart, but I knew they would cram at least another half a dozen people in. Finally the last place was filled by a large Ugandan women, who squeezed through the other passengers, sat on the empty seat next to me, and promptly dumped her young squalling baby on my lap. The driver appeared and slid into his seat, started the engine, and with loud revving, signalled for the tout and his mate to jump on board. After one last look around for passengers we were off.

A few hours later, halfway to Koboko, the unbelievably overcrowded minibus conked out. Kevin and I spent the next three hours explaining the principles of spark plug ignition to the driver. We didn't seem to be getting through to him.

"What do we do from here?" I asked Kevin. "How far is it to Koboko?"

"Oh, it's just over there," he said with understated flippancy as he pointed north.

"Fine," I said. "Let's walk."

"Are you nuts, *kwaja*?" he exclaimed, using the southern Sudanese word for 'white man'. "It's bloody dangerous around here."

It didn't look like it was dangerous, in fact it looked quite serene, but Kevin had been here and I hadn't so I deferred to his better judgement. So we started hitching, leaving the minibus driver to fiddle with a miasma of wires as the sun set.

We got a lift with what must have been the last vehicle heading north, but not before half the passengers from the minibus had transferred to the 4WD Toyota along with their sacks of produce.

Our driver, a Ugandan man with his wife, didn't seem at all perturbed by any real or imagined 'danger'. But he was clearly in a hurry. Despite the abominable state of the road, we arrived safely. So did the minibus. The next day we saw it in Koboko and wondered what magic the driver had worked up to coax the engine back to life.

In Koboko it soon became obvious that we had left the world of electricity (other than the occasional generator which shut down at 10pm), telephones, post, and stores that stock more than a few canned items, Coca-Cola and bottled beer behind. The town, however, is crawling with foreign NGOs ensconced in their own guarded compounds, complete with 'workers' oblivious to anything other than the prospect of a good hand in the card games they were always playing. The UN (World Food Programme) compound stands out in sharp contrast to the rest of the town's minimal facilities. Here, business cards, satellite TV, air-conditioning, new 4WDs and uniformed security guards rule the roost. Koboko does, however, have an air strip with twice weekly flights to and from Entebbe — demand permitting.

The main part of town is an eclectic combination of bland concrete blocks along two dusty streets, surrounded by *makuti*-roofed, mud-walled traditional houses. It's quite picturesque — if you ignore the idle aid relief trucks in their oil-spattered, tyre-strewn parking spots and the somewhat desperate Kenyan and Somali drivers waiting for the WFP to give them some work. Most of them said they had been doing nothing for months, despite the fact that the dry season was inexorably turning into the wet season, making travel by road difficult, if not impossible.

We stayed at the Swedish aid compound next door to the Hotel Delambience. It was superbly run by locals, and at US$10 a night with comfortable beds, mosquito nets, toilets, showers (which didn't work), full board and a smile, it was an absolute bargain. OK, so there was no drinking alcohol and no smoking allowed, but it did have radio contact with the towns we were aiming for — Yei and Maridi — over the border in Sudan.

The Delambience was equally pleasant and had a collection of makuti-roofed cottages surrounding a dining area and a somewhat dilapidated air-raid shelter behind the high white-washed walls. This was where you came if you wanted a beer. It was warm, but it was served with gusto and a mischievous grin by 'Mama'.

The next day we did the rounds of the NGOs and trucking companies in search of a lift across the Ugandan/Sudanese border at Kaya. Most maps don't show this border crossing, or even Koboko. While there were no buses or taxis heading in that direction, there were plenty of other forms of transport — as long as a bumpy ride, sandwiched like sardines on sacks of food was to your liking.

First we had to clear Ugandan customs. Every official at the border seemed to be carrying guns and the 'office' was a mud-floored shack with a rickety table and chair. Welcome to the war zone. At the border the locals just wandered through at will, and the customs officers weren't too bothered about protocol once they discovered we had a spare US$5 note and weren't carrying guns.

The first thing we saw at the bottom of the hill was a seriously rutted road in urgent need of repair and a gaggle of leaky tin-roofed shacks flying the flag of the New Sudan. We collected our rubber stamps and deftly dodged pointed requests for 'presents'. From here on our passports became redundant — everything revolved around the SRRA permit and the scrap of paper given to you by the Ugandan customs official.

Officials pulled out the grubby, dog-eared books and recorded our details in longhand. We were asked where we were going and what we planned to do. We gave them the answers we thought they wanted to hear. As an exercise in security it's little short of a joke, but we had to treat the situation with respect, despite the fact that no one seemed to be pushing the power of their pips or had the slightest interest in the contents of our bags.

Once we got through the red tape we zig-zagged to the top of the hill, past a wrecked tank which the local children used as a playground, and onto a plateau which gradually descended into the forest. The gravel road was remarkably good, the bridges less so. The forest — mainly teak trees — grew denser the closer we got to Yei. A number of massive granite outcrops livened up the view, but the wildlife was strangely absent — as it was when we went through the Murchison Falls National Park earlier in the journey. Fresh meat was obviously of primary interest to hungry soldiers armed with automatic weapons.

This whole region of north-western Uganda and southern Sudan was a no-go zone for many years after Idi Amin and, after him, Obote and the Okellos, were thrown out of Uganda by Yoweri Museveni's forces in the 80s. As the retreating forces fled north they devastated the area, taking everything they wanted whenever they wanted it. There were still reminders of that time, but a modest prosperity had returned to the area and the fields were again full of crops.

Suddenly we found ourselves in Yei and the reality of the war began to hit home — bombed-out buildings, pock-marked walls, fox-holes, air-raid shelters, no recognisable stores of any sort and SPLA soldiers sucking on beers in the town's only bar in anticipation of the next call to arms.

None of this prevented bureaucracy from grinding into action. The same old, grubby, dog-eared ledgers, pen-wielding officials asking awkward questions and, this time, restricted movement. Moving around town had to be done in the company of a trusted local person. In our case it was a young, well-spoken man from the aid compound who insisted on carrying our bags. He was very friendly and left us largely to our own devices.

Work on the new reinforced concrete air-raid shelter in the compound was well advanced. Concerned, we asked who would bomb us? Everybody was keen to answer our question: the Khartoum Government. The government's ageing Antonov bomber was based in Juba about 120km away to the north-east. The SPLA had taken Juba several times but had been unable to hang on to it. The exercise was more symbolic than anything else.

Luckily, everyone knew the Antonov flew low, made a lot of noise, was slow and its main target was the Norwegian People's Aid hospital for SPLA troops on the hill above town. In theory it meant you could virtually stroll to safety before the bombs dropped. The bomber's crew, however, were so inaccurate the bombs could land anywhere. Shrapnel was the biggest danger if you were foolish enough to remain above ground.

Sunday was the preferred bombing day — no doubt chosen to put the fear of God up the good Christians of the area. And then it happened. Lunch was abandoned as everyone hit their foxholes and shelters. Children screamed, women wailed, men uttered the foulest of curses and dogs howled. Fear was on everyone's faces as the bombs exploded.

"Jesus Christ! That was a bit close," Kevin shouted as shrapnel peppered the hatches of the shelter. A direct hit would have made mince-meat out of all of us. Surprisingly no one was killed and life resumed to normal as soon as the Antonov headed back to Juba. This was no Hollywood Vietnam movie. The SPLA didn't have any surface-to-air missiles or F111s. There were never going to be any firefights. In fact the locals seemed so inured to this fairly regular event that they were almost blasé about it.

Elsewhere around Yei you'd never have known a war was being fought. The forest plantations were well established, though neglected, and there were quite a few foreign aid projects involved in education, horticulture and the like. No-one was starving and there were no beggars, but the people were obviously poor. As outsiders, however, we needed cash for small purchases such as beer and cigarettes. This meant a pocketful of Ugandan shillings. No one used the almost worthless Sudanese pound, though you sometimes got the occasional note as change.

The main economic activity around Yei, other than growing food and fighting a war, was forestry. Teak forests in regimented rows stretched for miles. They had been planted, so we were told, by the British between the early 1900s and 1940s, but the pick of the trees had been felled and carted away in the late 50s and 60s following independence from Britain.

That night in Yei we were rewarded with an example of what rain meant in this part of the world. Within 30 minutes the sky was completely blacked out, lightning shattered the stillness and down came the rain — in torrents. We dashed, soaked to the skin, into the bar where the SPLA soldiers had been carousing two days earlier and sat drinking beer by candlelight as the rain swept everything before it.

In the morning, with the sun out again, there was nothing to show for the previous night's deluge except for a few puddles. We were worried, though, about how the bridges would hold up to this sort of punishment given their state of repair. It was time to move on before movement became impossible.

The next day we waited outside the customs post in the centre of town hoping that a food aid truck would come. A few hours later one eventually trundled through town.

The driver was headed for Maridi and his rig was a reliable Unimog semi-trailer. After going through the inevitable red tape and rubber stamp procedure yet again, we jumped in tthe cab and headed vaguely north-west. Our African driver clearly wasn't fazed by the possibility of rain. He looked as though he had done this trip many times, no doubt through hell and high water, and he clearly wanted to be back in Koboko as soon as possible. But this wasn't the relatively smooth driving which characterised the journey from Kaya to Yei.

The road worsened the further we got from Yei, but the driver took it all in his stride. Some of the bridges needed careful negotiation as many of their timbers were broken or had been knocked out of place. A wrong twist of the wheel or use of the brakes could have spelt catastrophe, a desperate swim to the bank and loss of the rig.

We finally made it to the local aid compund as darkness set in. They welcomed us warmly, but we knew this was their last outpost. The driver told us he was heading north, but the only contact name we had was for someone in Yambio — 120km to the west. It made no difference that he was the governor of Western Equatoria province, because we were quickly told he wasn't there. This was normal in SPLA-controlled territory. It's supposedly a security measure based on the supposition (or reality) that if you don't know where someone is then you can't do any damage.

Short of going there and finding out for ourselves, we were faced with the unenviable choice of heading south into Congo and then back to Arua in Uganda or backtracking to Yei. The entire north-east of Congo was a jigsaw of mutually antagonistic, well-armed militias who would probably shoot first and ask questions later. Ugandan and Rwandan regular forces were also involved. What a combination.

On top of that, we didn't have visas for the Congo — not that they would make any difference or guarantee that we'd be left standing with our dollars, mud-spattered shirts and sweaty boots intact.

There was no choice. We had to head back the way we'd just come. It is possible, of course, to get much closer to the front line — food aid trucks and UN light planes do it virtually every day — but the town of Rumbek would be our limit without prior agreement from various SPLA commanders or even the top man, Colonel John Garang.

How you would get over the front line, except in a body bag or in the company of Kofi Annan, was another matter entirely. Our main concern, however, were the rains which had set in with a vengeance.

The one thing in our favour was that trucks heading back to Uganda would be empty, so they would be unlikely to snap already weakened bridge timbers. The first lift we got, however, was in a pick-up which turned back after 30km, leaving us in a village where local people thought we were aid workers and pestered us for goodies. We didn't have any. All we had were a few cigarettes, which quickly disappeared.

The village was fairly typical for this part of Africa — just a cluster of mud-walled, makuti-roofed huts off to one side of the road, and, like many others, it had a school with basic facilities and plenty of children milling around, some of whom had a smattering of English.

"So now what, *bwana*?" I asked Kevin as we shared our last smoke.

"We wait. Do you have any other brilliant ideas?"

I didn't, but several hours later a returning food aid truck skidded to a halt after some manic gesturing on our part in the middle of the muddy road. Relieved, we jumped on board. We reached Yei by nightfall. Once again the rain was bucketing down.

Two days later we were told our contact from Yambio was in town. He wasn't. Then we were told he'd gone to Arua.

It was time to hit the road again. There was simply too much military activity in this part of the world for comfort, and the next day we negotiated a lift in the back of a pick-up to Koboko. It was a pity to have achieved what seemed to be so little, but we were not in any sort of reasonable bargaining position.

Strangely, we ran into our Yambio contact in Arua. It seemed like a waste of time, but we went along with the customary exchange of litre bottles of Johnny Walker Black Label, even though they should have been consumed in Yambio.

The next day saw us back in Kampala, but not before a hold-up at Packwach due to 'military contingencies'. Obviously the area wasn't as secure as we'd thought, but the hold-up had its benefits. It resulted in a large traffic jam of buses and trucks which, in turn, meant we'd essentially travelled in convoy back to the main road running south to Kampala.

So did we achieve anything other than rekindle our memories of tramping through the African bush?

Well, yes and no. To call it 'intrepid' was stretching a point since we relied on public transport or the trucks and pick-ups of aid organisations, but it was far from what most Westerners would regard as 'normal' civilisation where most things are available at the flip of a switch and where you don't have to dash to the cover of an air-raid shelter every week.

We did return to find that not a great deal had changed, and was unlikely to change soon if the snail's pace of peace negotiations between the warring factions was anything to go by.

Still, I guess discomfort, hassles and danger have their own reward if the excited chatter of overland travellers gathering in various bars in Nairobi, Harare or Cape Town is anything to go by.

But they can go home and resume a 'normal' life. The rest of us stay here, dealing with realities and preparing for the next influx of 'adventurers'. There's nothing wrong with that — I spent decades doing the same sort of thing all over the world — but there is a point at which you have to connect: the point at which encounter becomes commitment and commitment becomes your life.

Being 'intrepid' is a phase we all go through when we're young and rootless. It's fun. Then you have to get your arse in gear.

Riding to Timbuktu and back

by Colin Field

I n Burkina Faso, the days had become stiflingly hot. The small dusty road we'd chosen was nothing like it appeared on the map. It was smaller. The villages were nearly non-existent, with less infrastructure than I could have possibly imagined. The sun beat down ferociously, devouring any good humour we possessed. Bridges had been washed away, food was difficult to get, and water was always a tad dodgy. We were looking forward to our arrival in Ouagadougou. The coast of Ghana was now a million miles away, and I was thinking one mile at a time.

It was pure stupidity to cycle during the heat of the day, yet as usual we'd learned the hard way. Arriving at villages yb mid-afternoon, the sun shining with a whiteness that threatened to envelope our wearied selves, we'd search around for something sugary to kick-start our bodies, before collapsing in any shade available. Eyes stared the entire time. We swore not to travel at that time of day again.

Towards the end of the road to Ouaga we began riding by moonlight to avoid the sun. Concentrating steadily on the bumpy laterite road ahead, the moon hazily inadequate, our minds sifted through dreams, eager for sleep and yet anxious to cover as much ground as possible.

We passed through the peaceful darkness of mudbrick villages alight with the glow of weak bulbs or lanterns. Ghostlike figures meandered by, casually busy; cooking, gathering, joking. At times the rhythms of Africa immemorial were drummed out upon *djembes*, breaking the silence with earthy songs of old.

Travis, my travel companion, was the most unlikely of partners. During his first days in Ghana he was wide-eyed and lost, bumbling around in a daze of culture shock. Fresh from the Canadian winter, he was pastily clean shaven. Surprisingly, he was the one who convinced me to ride to Timbuktu. I thought it would be cool to spend New Year there, and he was keen to go by bicycle. The man couldn't mend a puncture, though. We soon found him a bike in Makola market in Accra, some children's panniers, and were good to go. We turned out to be a great match, and his relaxed attitude helped us out of many a jam and made the trip as enjoyable as the struggle could be.

Somewhere along the road I had the painful experience of watching Travis repair a punctured tube. I was sick of constantly being the mechanic, and he needed to learn how to do it, so I watched, relaxing in the shade of a baobab as he prepared to repair it. Getting the wheel off was the first big obstacle; he fumbled around, struggling to free the wheel from the chain. That done, he began removing the tyre and carried on with the job. I suppose he didn't do too badly, but what should really have taken five minutes ended up taking about 45. Time enough for the sun to reach its apex and our water supply to become low. I was frustrated with his pace, but said nothing, as his new-found skills were, no doubt, developing.

I knew that when we parted ways he would do all right. Though his mechanical abilities were lacking, his inability to get angry really inspired respect. The people of Africa admire this kind of quiet calm from foreigners. In any slightly awkward situation his relaxed manner would soon win over the kindness of the aggressor. Whether we were arguing about prices or the need for a guide, Travis' social skills would always be victorious and we would come out winners. He was the perfect companion, positive and full of laughs. It was no vacation, though. We'd made it to Timbuktu in time for a magical New Year and were now returning the way we'd come.

The 400km piste took us eight days, from San in Mali, to Ouagadougou, Burkina Faso. It was perhaps one of the most challenging roads I have yet to encounter. It was entirely off any kind of tourist track, and probably off any kind of bush-taxi route too. Ancient bridges had been washed away in past rainy seasons. We were constantly having mechanical problems: the bumpy road played havoc with our wheels, and punctures and broken spokes were a daily annoyance.

We later met a Dutch couple cycling from London to Cape Town who had done five kilometres of this road before turning back. They were impressed at our feat, and we were thankful to have someone who understood our accomplishment.

It's funny how much relativity plays a part in one's view of a city. The first time through Ouaga I was fresh from London. Ouagadougou seemed like a sorry excuse for civilisation. Yet now, after Mali, this was my Mecca.

My first impression of the city had been of a lively one, all dusty and noisy with mobylettes and bicycles plying the roadside, while vehicles whisked quickly between them, undisturbed by the surrounding ordered chaos. I thought the place had a feeling of post-apocalyptic decrepitude. The incessant dust and pollution from straining two-stroke engines had greyed all structures with hues of black and brown, as if fallout had at one time covered the city in a deathlike veil. Former president Sankara had some strange architectural fetishes, and gigantic blocks of filthy concrete are scattered throughout the city, all in various states of disrepair. I had seen ancient beggars with pollution-soaked clothes and misty blind eyes, hissing at passing whites, holding out their jingling tins in hopes of recognition.

Now, however, after eight days on a dusty rural road, Ouagadougou was an entirely different experience for me. The liveliness was welcome, and the Lebanese restaurants and supermarkets were like great kingdoms of familiar foods. I bought a Mars Bar and devoured it happily, wondering if it was the chocolate or the civilisation I craved.

Thankfully, the road leaving Ouaga was paved. The sky was filled with the dusty Harmattan winds that blow in the Saharan sands, fogging the air with a yellowish haze. A rural landscape bordered the road. A dry yellow seemed to conquer all; crumbly mud huts were scattered along the road, and circular buildings with thatched roofs were all linked into compounds with walls of mud. Some nights we stayed with these farmers in the rural countryside. Approaching humbly we would attempt to communicate in either French or English. If neither were understood we would resort to sign language. Two palms pressed together and held at the side of a leaning head meant sleep. This usually got the point across. Making a triangle symbol represented our tent and we would then be shown where we could set up. The family would invariably surround us, fascinated at our equipment.

By staying at isolated farms we avoided the excited eyes that would surround us when we stayed in villages. After a long day of cycling, the last thing we had the energy for was socialising. Having to ask the chief if we could stay in the village, then being surrounded by curious, smiling children was exhausting. Although a great experience, we just weren't up for it at times.

The farms, on the other hand, were a relaxing and peaceful alternative. We never asked for food, although without fail we would be offered some rice or *fufu* or whatever it was the family were eating that night. Joining the family in the compound, we would look at each other, uncomfortable, giggling. Farmers were very rarely well educated, so they had learned neither French nor English, but their eyes gleamed and their children were infatuated with us. The hospitality was incredible, and having little to offer them, we usually gave them a little money and bowed with thanks in the morning before heading on our way.

On other nights we would find a hidden spot behind some trees and pitch our tent for the night. Africans thought we were crazy to do this. Their fear of *djinns* had not been dispelled by the influx of foreign religions, and for them, the bush was full of spirits. One particular night, having just passed through a small village, we searched for a spot in the bush to camp. It was difficult to find a site in the dark, but we soon found what we were looking for, set up and laid down to sleep. Beneath the stars, exhausted, dreams quickly overtook us.

In the morning we awoke to the sounds of footsteps and yelling. Startled, we emerged from the tent quickly to find we were being approached by two police officers. We had made the mistake of setting up camp on the *Gendarmerie* property. The officers were not impressed and two of them quickly sized us up, realising we were probably good bribe victims. Travis brought out his trusty smile, though, apologising as they thoroughly examined our passports. Showing our visa stamps for the countries we had passed through, we explained that we were travelling by bicycle. They looked at us in disbelief and could no longer keep up the stern act. They began to smile. Fascinated, they watched as we packed our things, asking curious questions and wishing us luck as we rode off, fine-free.

Bicycles themselves are not an unfamiliar sight in this area of the world, but a white person on a bicycle was. The response to us was always different, but always positive. In the mornings, as women collected water from stagnant pools, great heavy buckets on their heads, walking in friendly groups, they would stare at us in disbelief. So often the only white people they see are speeding past in air-conditioned 4WDs. One old woman, all wrinkled and leathery with age, dropped to her knees and bowed as if to Allah upon seeing us. She garbled away in the local tongue and her friends held their bellies with laughter. So did I.

Passing vehicles were a constant concern. In many places the road had jagged edges where soil erosion had taken great bite-shaped chunks out of the road, leaving foot-high drops which were dangerous to the wheels of a fully loaded bicycle. A loud honk from behind would tell us to get off the road. We would oblige. A borrowed guidebook had warned us about this danger, and advised us to put rear-view mirrors on our helmets. We laughed at the suggestion of helmets. Other travellers always asked if we wore them, and were invariably surprised at out negative answer. People thought we were crazy. Of course we were crazy. We were riding bicycles through West Africa. What a stupid idea.

In the daytime we would often pass African cyclists. Old men, young boys, doubled up, groups of young girls, all going to school or market, or coming from them. As I caught up with them from behind they would turn to see me, startled. I always smiled at their flabbergasted expressions.

The young men didn't like to be passed, and would give chase on their ancient one-speed Chinese bicycles. They would never lose me. I remember a few of them hitting 40 kilometres an hour. After a few minutes of this they would turn off to go home, yelling "*merci monsieur!*" with big smiles on their faces.

The main difficulty with bicycle touring in the Sahel is carrying enough water. We often had nine litres between the two of us, but even so, by the time we reached somewhere to buy water we were parched with thirst. Nine litres is also an enormous weight which, although necessary, puts great strain on the bicycle. Combine the weight with a bad bumpy road, and mechanical failure is inevitable. But there is no way around it. Large quantities of water are essential. Maps can only tell you so much, and you can never be sure how large the next village will be, and whether or not they will have drinkable water.

Knowing we were leaving French Africa, however, I couldn't resist packing my panniers with beautiful French baguettes. I wasn't looking forward to Ghanaian tea bread. Unfortunately years of British colonisation in Ghana hadn't left a great tradition of bread makers behind.

Crossing into Ghana involved one formality after another. Border guards put on serious expressions upon our arrival. Very serious stuff. Checking papers, entry stamps and filling out forms which ask for your mother's maiden name. It was always a little intimidating at first, but it took very little time to have them smiling the great grins I loved to see.

"*Tous par velo*?"

"*Oui*," I would reply.

"*Vous êtes fou!*" — 'You are crazy!'

Like the policemen before, they treated us with a strange kind of respect and joked around with us, as if all the seriousness of their jobs had been forgotten and whisked away. On both sides of the Burkina Faso/Ghana border we were received with wide-eyed amazement, grins, handshakes and good wishes for the future. I swear you can get away with anything if you arrive at a border on a bicycle.

Our Ghanaian goal was Tamale, where some of my old university mates were working on development projects. Arriving in Tamale was refreshing. I soon found my friends, and just like on our first time through town, we indulged ourselves in a few cool drinks. It was Saturday night, so we headed off to the local bar, Old Timers, and danced the night away to the Ghanaian sounds of Daddy Lumba. Travis and I stayed with Katie and Jean, who were both working on the Guinea Worm Eradication Project (GWEP). It was a treat to have a place to stay and a stove to cook on.

However, the morning once againfound me with what I called the 'deathly lethargy'. The first tell-tale symptom of malaria. It was the worst type of déjà vu. The first time through Tamale. I'd woken one morning with a hangover that wouldn't quit. And the lethargy. Travis had dragged me off to the hospital, which was a frightening experience in itself. Goats sauntered around the dusty open air building, scratching themselves on the edge of a fountain that probably never worked.

Blood smears confirmed that the Lariam wasn't working. We both had malaria. The doctor was soon giving us shots of choloroquine, chuckling at the white folk who considered malaria to be dangerous. They spend most of their lives dealing with this terrible disease. We were given a prescription for about five different kinds of medicine which we later found out prevented worms and other totally unrelated diseases. To the African, the more pills the better.

The memories of the hospital turned me off this time around, so I went to the local lab and had a blood smear and a stool sample. Katie and Jean had become experts at self diagnosis, and their guesstimation was malaria and amœbic dysentery. We self-prescribed the relevant drugs, bought them at the pharmacy and began waiting for me to feel better. I lay upon the bed in a state of complete fatigue, enduring the heat with the help of a squeaky fan and as many bucket showers as I could muster up the energy to take.

Travis needed to get going, and since I was safe amongst friends, he decided it was time for him to hit the road alone. He was planning to ride to Mole game reserve, and then on to the coast for some relaxation before his flight back to the Canadian winter. The thought of cycling alone from here on in was both frightening and exciting. Solo travel is true freedom, and although I knew I had some recovering to do I looked forward to being alone. I watched him ride off on the dusty road and cringed as I heard his grinding gears shift noisily.

During my recovery I became interested in the programme Katie and Jean were involved in. Guinea worm is one of those diseases people who have never been to Africa will warn you about before your trip. Contracted from coming into contact with contaminated water, the worm is a parasite that lives in a host's body. Once inside, it can achieve lengths of up to 120cm before emerging from a blister, normally found on the lower extremities. Symptoms can range from pain and itching to the inability to walk for up to three months, yet there is no known drug that can kill the worm without harming the victim.

Eradication is possible if human hosts avoid contact with contaminated water supplies, and GWEP is attempting to do this through educational drama. After recovering from my own bout of illnesses, Henry, the local coordinator of GWEP, took me to one of the rural villages just west of Tamale. Through Jean and Katie's surveying we knew there were two people in the village suffering from the disease. The village was a dry African red, where walls and paths blended in a uniform shade of mud.

We found the two infected boys and I watched in both horror and amazement as Henry skilfully cut into the blister and removed the worm.

It was about a foot long and looked like a long wet piece of spaghetti. The next boy wasn't so lucky. The blister was up near his testicles and removal was impossible.

My departure date was quickly approaching and I had a long way to go before I would arrive at the coast. I was looking forward to a week of rest on the beach before returning to the fast pace of London. I was much healthier, and after a heartfelt goodbye to Katie and Jean I headed south, coast-bound.

Leaving Tamale was difficult. After months on the road, two weeks in one place had made it feel somewhat like home. Familiar faces are probably the thing you miss most when on the road, and I had made some great friends and people who had really touched my heart. The Africans I met really have an interest in foreigners and the rumours of fantastic Ghanaian hospitality are all true.

As far as tourist attractions go, West Africa doesn't really have any. There are few truly awe-inspiring natural wonders, but it is the people that make the countries of West Africa so inviting. They are so eager to meet foreigners and learn about the wider world. Chance meetings can turn into great friendships, and these are the tales that get related upon return. Not the great sights or spectacular scenery, but the lives of the people who live in this fascinating part of the dark continent. The people are so willing to bring you into their lives, to introduce you to their families and friends, to invite you into their home for meals and lodgings, to treat you as a guest and to give you some part of the little they have. West Africa is not about planned events. It is the chance encounters that make it so magical.

The road south was hilly and winding, making progress slow and disheartening. The road wasn't very busy, and villages were scattered sporadically at comfortable distances, making the cycling easy and manageable. At police roadblocks they would look through my passport and tell me that Travis had passed through a week earlier. He seemed to be covering incredible distances.

I had been having wheel problems the entire trip and as I rolled into a small town I heard the all too familiar pop! pop! of spokes breaking. I soon met a young teenager who helped me find a room for the night and promised to return in the morning to help me fix my bike. I was grateful and fell asleep instantly in my small cube of a room.

True to his word the boy returned early the next morning and took me to see his friend the bicycle repairman. Twisted branches held up the thatched roof of the repair shack, and although the man spoke neither French nor English, we managed to communicate. The broken spokes were on the same side as the chain and I needed to remove the rear cog in order to put new spokes in. I didn't have the tool, and neither did he. But he wasn't fazed. With a hammer and a screwdriver, it was soon apart with little springs and ball bearings falling onto the dirt floor. I've worked at a bike store for years and I have never seen anyone take a freewheel apart and attempt to put it back together. It's just not worth the effort. I watched, amazed, wondering if this guy actually knew what he was doing. I wondered if I should go and book a room for another night.

Within half an hour, with about six men all standing around discussing how to put the thing back together, they had done it. I was amazed. New spokes, a straight wheel and a functional rear cog.

They charged me a pittance.

As I was leaving I asked the boy who had helped me find the room and the repairman if I could buy him a soda for his troubles.

He said, "No. I'm Muslim. I don't drink soda."

"Oh," I said, thinking it a strange answer. "Can I buy you a malt then?"

"I want beer."

I bought him a small beer and asked him why he could drink beer and not soda. He ignored my question. He chugged it back and then rode with me for about ten kilometres, giggly and happy. I felt a twinge of guilt at having corrupted the poor lad, but soon settled into the saddle for another day of awaiting downhills and the soothing sound of my freewheel clicking away effortlessly. African mechanics can fix anything.

People always say to me that travel by bicycle must be a rewarding experience. I don't usually look at it as rewarding, although I suppose, in hindsight it is. It is certainly challenging, both mentally and physically, and it is an incredibly absorbing way to see the country one visits.

Little villages, which from a bus seem like painted images on the bus window, become, on a bicycle, tangible reality. A chance to rest, to meet people, to eat, to sleep. And you see the village. Its people become concrete, the memory indelible. The transition from rural to urban is not only seen but experienced. It is as close to being fully independent as one can be without owning a car. No longer is the traveller reliant upon the schedules of buses and bush-taxis, and their cramped, boiling interiors become but a memory. Any road, piste or trail is open for exploration, and getting off the beaten path becomes a daily experience. I can no longer imagine going anywhere without a bicycle.

Even despite the humidity, arriving at the coast was such a relief. Heading to my favourite little beach resort just west of Accra, I settled in for a vacation. A week of nothing but beach, booze and contemplation. I felt I'd earned it.

The long road north

by Liz Durno

It was raining hard as we backed out the driveway, locked the gate and headed north from our home in Johannesburg. Not the best start to our African adventure, but it was late autumn and we weren't really expecting a downpour.

It had been a long year and the promise of this three-week break had been keeping us going for the past few months. All the preparations were made, we'd had our yellow fever jabs, were fully stocked with malaria prophylactics, our Chev Nomad was loaded to the roof, James our boerbul-bul mastiff (with state vet clearance) was breathing down our necks from the back and there was nothing but the open road ahead of us.

Having already seen quite a bit of Zimbabwe, we decided to approach our final destination of Zambia differently and travel through Botswana instead. A country of stark beauty, I summed it up in just two words — flat and donkeys. We didn't see many animals except for the donkeys which abounded along the roadside throughout the country. That's not to say there isn't wildlife. The Tswana are very proud of their heritage and, realising the value of ecotourism, do everything they can to protect their wildlife for the lucrative tourist trade.

Botswana is almost uniformly flat, with 85% of its area covered by the semi-arid Kalahari. The rest is an almost roadless expanse of savannahs, wetlands and salt pans with the population living mostly in a narrow corridor in the east.

We were travelling on a shoestring budget, so had come fully prepared to rough it when necessary. The rain had finally let up so we drove as far as Seruli, pulled over to the side of the road just outside town and set up camp. James was extremely pleased to be able to run around again. Not being in a camping area, we didn't light a fire but cooked on gas under the starry sky and turned in for the night.

We were woken by birdsong in the morning and crawled out of our tent into a rather chilly morning. Even in midsummer the mornings and evenings were pretty cold due to Botswana's desert climate.

By midday, however, we were baking in the car and James was panting out of the window. Things got a little hair-raising when he started looking for a cool place to lie down and decided it looked nice and shady next to my feet. I don't know if you've ever tried to drive with 25kg of puppy lying on your feet but, take it from me, it's not possible. I coasted over to the side of the road, switched off the engine, and David and I spent the next ten minutes trying to coax a reluctant dog out of what he considered the ideal spot for a siesta.

We drove through Francistown and Nata and stopped at Kasane, the northern tip of the Chobe National Park and the park's gateway and administrative centre. We took a drive along the riverfront where the bulk of the park's animals congregate and were awed by the destruction wreaked by the elephant population, who had left the riverfront looking like a bombsite.

We stayed in Kasane that night and, when we got to the border at Kazangula bright and early the next morning, the cars were already queueing to catch the ferry over to Zambia. The Zambezi River rises in the west of the country and forms the border between Zambia and Namibia, Botswana and Zimbabwe. We waited in glorious sunshine next to the car while James frolicked around in the shallows of Zambia's main river. He was having a great time till one of the ferry operators hurried over to warn us that someone's dog had been taken by a crocodile just the week before. David quickly wrestled him out of the water and he spent the rest of the wait firmly tied up on his leash.

At last our turn came and we trundled onto the ferry along with another two vehicles. We got across to the other side without incident and waited patiently to get through the border post. We'd learnt long ago, that accepting before you even begin your trip that nothing is going to happen quickly, will save a lot of frustration, and ensure a great time.

Clutching our passports with our visas eventually stamped, we hurried back to the car and set off for one of the highlights of our holiday — the two-kilometre-wide, 100m-high Victoria Falls. Named Mosi-oa-Tunya by the locals it was not hard to see how it earned the title 'The Smoke that Thunders'. Being early May, it was just after the rainy season and the falls were in full flow — a truly awesome sight. We took a guided tour around the falls and over the spindly walkways perched over the abyss. The swirling clouds of spray keep everything well soaked, and we had to be careful not to slip. The spray is so thick it looks as if it is raining upwards.

In Zambia we enjoyed different views of the Victoria Falls from those usually seen on the better-known Zimbabwean side. For those wanting an entirely different view, there's always the 111m bungee jump from the Victoria Falls Bridge. It's the longest bungee in the world. We weren't feeling quite that brave. We ended the day soaked to the skin, exhilarated and refreshed.

We pushed on the next morning, through Choma, Mazabuka and Kafue till we got to Lusaka. Although it is the capital, I wouldn't recommend spending more time in Lusaka than you have to. A city that didn't even exist before the 20th century, it has mushroomed at an uncontrollable pace with two million of the country's population of nine million inhabiting one of the fastest-growing cities in central Africa. Well over 60% of its inhabitants are unemployed, but there are surprisingly few beggars. As everywhere, petty theft occurs, but most people try to make an honest living, selling their wares or services and smiling to boot.

While violent crime is not usual, you do have to be aware of your surroundings at all times and to watch your possessions like a hawk. I was lounging in the passenger seat of the car while David was in the bank, when my door was wrenched open by a would-be thief. He merely apologised profusely when he realised there was someone sitting in the car.

Some other travellers we met told us how they too had been waiting in their car for their companions. A man kept tapping on their window and telling them to look under their car but they steadfastly ignored him, thinking it was a ruse to get them out of the car. When their companions returned, a handful of street kids scattered from under the car where they had been unbolting anything that would come off — number plates, spare tyres, the works.

David took forever in the bank — which can be blamed on the Zambian currency. The kwacha, which in 1995 was about 2,000 to the British pound, had since plummeted, and we were getting closer to 5,000. We became instant millionaires the minute we converted our sterling. The drawbacks of this come when paying for expensive items, and many people use a briefcase to carry cash — a wallet just won't do the trick. Local farmers we spoke to joked that they would indicate how much items cost by holding their thumb and forefinger apart to show how many notes were needed.

David found it less of a joke when he got stuck in a queue in the bank behind companies wanting to deposit their day's takings. The security guard from the Holiday Inn had two wheeled suitcases full of notes.

Business concluded, we decided to experience how the local masses shop by heading to Lusaka's markets. We breathed in the colourful and lively atmosphere of the bustling Soweto Market. There was a confusing mixture of items and services on sale, from bales of second hand clothing from the West (known as *salaula*) to *chitengis* (brightly coloured cotton sarongs) to dried fish and fresh vegetables, hairdressers and motor spares dealers.

After bargaining (nothing has a fixed price) for the two chitengis I wanted, we headed back to the car which was surprisingly still intact, although that probably had more to do with James, who was sitting inside, than blind luck.

After a spot of culture at the Henry Tayali Visual Arts Gallery we decided to call it a day, so we headed for a campsite we'd passed on our way into Lusaka

Eureka farm is about ten kilometres south of Lusaka on the Kafue Road and, as with so many other farms, has branched out into hospitality. They have a campsite, ablution facilities and a thatched *sitenje* with a bar, lounge and pool table for entertainment.

We pitched our tent and headed straight for the bar to down a couple of ice-cold Mosi beers. I had accumulated more than enough travel dust by now to warrant a shower. I was met by a Belgian woman pressed up against the wall whimpering in fear about something scary in the shower block. I tiptoed in in trepidation, only to find a praying mantis eyeing me from the safety of the shower curtain. In spite of all my reassurances, I was unable to convince the Belgian that it was safe to shower, so enjoyed having the showers to myself — insects aside.

I emerged to see that a convoy of vehicles had arrived at the campsite. Three five-ton Bedford lorries and a one-ton utility van towing various trailers, tractors, farming implements and a caravan were taking up a sizeable chunk of the campsite.

The Sherriffs were a family of South African farmers looking for a better life in Zambia. After 27 years of being put through the wringer by Kenneth Kaunda, Zambians voted for democracy and Frederick Chiluba came to power in 1991. With him he brought all sorts of incentives to attract foreign investment and regain favour with the World Bank and IMF. Part of his plan was to attract farming expertise to the country by offering virgin land on a 99-year leasehold, imported farming materials to be duty free and the ability to keep a percentage of profits made in foreign exchange. The Sherriffs were just one of many farming families who decided to leave the uncertainty of South Africa and start anew. It had taken them ten days to get from Johannesburg to Lusaka and they still had a couple more days to go to get to their farm in central Zambia.

The parents and their two 20-something sons were prepared to start from scratch, clearing virgin land, planting crops, making bricks, building houses — basically modern-day pioneering. We wished them luck as we set off the next morning heading north at a slightly faster rate than the top speed of 50kph that their Bedfords could manage.

We negotiated our way through Lusaka, weaving round enormous roundabouts and through traffic lights that everyone seemed to ignore, before we got clear of the city and started heading up the Great North Road.

We saw big bags of charcoal piled all along the roadside waiting for collection by the trucks that would take them to market. We also saw the devastation caused by the charcoal industry where once densely forested areas have been decimated.

We weren't able to spend too much time admiring the scenery though, as all our concentration was focused on the road and avoiding the potholes, some of which spanned the road so you had to drive on the verge to get round them. We had thought the farmer at Eureka was exaggerating when he said it was a standing Zambian joke that if you saw a pair of ears sticking out of a pothole, you shouldn't mistakenly think it was a rabbit. It was far more likely to be a donkey. These potholes were big.

As if the roads weren't enough to contend with, there were also the other drivers. Our guidebook warned us that '*If you haven't driven in Africa before, this is no place to start*'. Officially, all you need to drive in Zambia is an international driver's licence. What would also be handy is nerves of steel. Driving is officially on the left, but you have to drive defensively and be prepared for anything.

We took turns driving north, passing through Kabwe and Kapiri Mposhi where the Tazara railway line from Dar es Salaam in the north meets the Zambian railway from the south, and goods and passengers have to change lines and stations.

The Great North Road has regular roadblocks manned by army personnel. Apparently they are there to check for stolen vehicles headed for the Democratic Republic of Congo, whose border is very close to the road south of Serenje. We stopped at one roadblock and, while a soldier was checking our papers, the truck in front of us decided to make tracks. As soon as they pulled off, another soldier went sprinting across the road whistling loudly, a police car came screaming out of a side road and five of them piled in and set off in hot pursuit.

At the same roadblock on our return journey south, a three-ton lorry roared past without stopping. Without hesitation, one of the soldiers let fly with his Russian Uzi — pop, pop, pop. The lorry went from 100kph to nought in about two seconds. We didn't stick around to see what happened next.

There are no such things as public toilets on the open road (or even in the towns for that matter) so when nature calls you answer wherever you happen to be. I would crouch very discreetly behind scrubby bushes on the side of the road, well out of sight of passing cars — though not out of sight, I discovered, of passing trucks which had a bird's-eye view of my undignified scramble to preserve my modesty.

On one of these stops I discovered the strangest specimen of nature. I heard a sort of screeching noise and traced the sound to a blob of jelly that looked remarkably like a large chicken dropping. James noticed it too, and every time he tried to sniff it, it let out a load wail exactly like the air coming out of a balloon when you pull the neck tight. On closer inspection, it turned out to be a frog — the 'chicken turd' having spindly arms and legs sticking out at each end. It had secreted some kind of goo and, with dried leaves stuck all over it, was extremely well camouflaged.

We eventually left it in peace, but it could have come straight out of a Gerald Durrell book.

We stopped off in Mkushi, a well-established farming block, and got chatting to some locals who suggested we stop for the night and come to their clubhouse for a few drinks. We were happy to oblige and whiled away a pleasant evening finding out how commercial farmers who hadn't fled Kaunda's rule had fared.

We pulled into Serenje to fill the car and our jerry cans with petrol and I couldn't help thinking about the Sherriffs, for whom this dusty one-horse town was to be their final destination.

I popped into the butcher's shop to see if I could get some meat to vary our diet of tinned and packet food, but quailed at the sight of the flies and the two cow's legs crossed nonchalantly on the counter.

Mrs Molelo, the butcher's wife, took pity on me and directed me across the road to one of the general dealers' stores where I stocked up on potatoes, tomatoes, pumpkin and onions. Strangely, I didn't really feel like eating meat any more.

While David was waiting for petrol, he got chatting to a tall American man in his 60s, complete with dungarees, straw hat and a friendly "How y'all doin".

He was Tom Waddell, an American missionary who had been living in Zambia with his wife Lucille for 25 years. The Waddells taught the locals sustainable farming practices at a farm, slightly north of Serenje, which was owned by their Baptist church. The farm would be handed over to the Zambians to manage when the couple retired back to the States.

Tom invited us to their place for lunch and we were treated to corn on the cob and 'tamaters' followed by pecan pie and a tour of the farm. By the time we left, the car was loaded with bananas, eggs, strawberries and various other home grown produce to see us on our way.

We pushed on through Mpika, making our way to the chalets at the Kapishya Hot Springs. There were campsites as well so we set up on the banks of the Manshya River next to an old farmhouse and made our way down to the hot springs. Crystal clear hot waters bubbled up through the rock and sand surrounded by lush vegetation and palm trees. I found it a bit disconcerting at first as my feet sank into the coarse sand all the way up to the knees before hitting bedrock. We wallowed for almost an hour till our fingers looked like prunes and our strength was totally sapped by the heat, and then had a relaxed dinner in the old farmhouse before collapsing for the night.

We woke up feeling thoroughly invigorated and took advantage of the excess energy to do a week's worth of hand-washing which we left to dry while we went exploring.

Stewart Gore-Brown, a young British officer, came out to Zambia in 1911 to determine the border between Northern Rhodesia and the Belgian Congo. He fell so in love with the place that he was determined to come back and settle once his work was finished. He was back in 1914 and purchased 10,000 acres of land near the Ishiba Ng'andu — the 'Lake of the Royal Crocodile' — for two shillings an acre and called it Shiwa Ng'andu. The First World War necessitated a return to England, but he was back six years later to set about building his estate.

It was quite an uncanny experience wandering among the thoroughly English buildings. Cottages for workers, a school, chapel, hospital, post office and workshop complex were built all those years ago, by locally recruited and trained builders, carpenters and blacksmiths, and using local materials. Gore-Brown later built an airstrip, and eventually the elaborate 72-room manor house overlooking the lake was completed in 1932. Gore-Brown's family continues to play a central role in the development of local farming, providing resources and expertise to local farmers.

We started our southward trek the next morning. I might have known our luck was too good to last. We had our first puncture of the trip just south of Mpika and although we had seen signs in Kabwe proclaiming '*punches repaired here*', we were on our own and had to change the tyre. While we were battling with jacks and wheel nut spanners, a 4WD utility van pulled over and a big burly man dressed in khaki with a bushy beard and twinkling blue eyes got out to enquire if he could help.

Kobus Wagenaar, another South African farmer who had settled in Zambia, was on his way to town to go shopping with his 89-year-old mother, Tant Jessie. She didn't wear glasses or use a walking stick and was less than impressed at being dragged thousands of miles from South Africa to live out her dotage in the middle of nowhere. We chatted for a while and, once they had seen that we'd be OK, they went on their way.

You have to be fully prepared to do bush mechanics while travelling on Zambia's roads, because even if you don't have an accident, the potholes are enough to rattle things loose. We hit one particularly hard bump, which finished off the end section of our exhaust. We didn't realise what had happened till every light in the car stopped working. The heat from the exhaust had fused all the wires together, blown all the fuses and shorted out the indicator and hazard control. We had to get the whole car rewired and ended up with separate switches for left and right indicators, which we had to click on and off manually when we needed hazard lights.

The final straw came when David slammed the bonnet after filling the radiator with water — the headlights came on and would only go off when we switched them on.

We drove south as far as Kabwe and, while filling up with petrol, met New Zealand missionary Dave Salisbury and his family. They invited us to go to one of the villages with them to see the work they do. The Zambians are wonderfully hospitable people who will share the little they have with total strangers. Although there are 73 different tribes and about 35 different languages spoken, most Zambians, no matter how rural, will have a rudimentary knowledge of English. The accents take a little getting used to as the Zambians tend to swop the letters 'r' and 'l'. Once I'd got that worked out, I quite understood when they told me that people get 'maralia' in the 'lainy' season.

We ate around the fire, rolling the stiff maize meal porridge called *nshima* into balls and dipping it into the tomato relish. You have to be careful with nshima as it is very hot and sticks to your fingers, as David found out when he was a little too enthusiastic in dipping his hand into the pot. After dinner, Dave Salisbury and his team set up their screen, put the speakers on the top of the 4WD, lugged the generator off into the bushes and showed the film *Jesus* translated into Bemba. This was quite a remarkable experience considering the simplicity of lives lived 2000 years ago, and the simple life of rural Zambians today. We camped at the village that night and said our farewells in the morning before resuming the long trek south.

At Fringilla Guest House in Chisamba, 60km north of Lusaka, we were made to feel right at home by Andrew Woodley, the owner. He invited us to stick around and join their boat-building party in his workshop where we made a raft out of 44-gallon drums.

The next day, the whole Chisamba community and a lot of farming families from the Lusaka area got together at Kulangwa Farm outside Chisamba. It was a full day with an 'Anything That Floats' competition (a lot of them didn't), a fishing competition, a big *braai* for lunch and a lot of socialising in general. All the money raised went towards putting a roof on the Chisamba clinic.

We were in no condition to drive any further that day so we spent a second night at Fringilla. On our way to the bar late that afternoon, we saw a microlight circling overhead. We thought no more of it till a man in a flying suit appeared. GPS strapped to his leg and helmet under his arm, he made quite an odd sight. He turned out to be part of a Norwegian team flying their microlights from Cape Town to Norway — Cape to North Cape — and simply wanted permission to spend the night on the farm.

We were off again in the morning, only to experience one more little bit of car trouble. I heard a 'snap' and the accelerator hit the floor. We just gained speed and I couldn't brake or change gears as it just over-revved. All I could do was switch off and coast over to the side of the road where David discovered the accelerator spring had broken. Luckily it wasn't too serious and we were on the move again in about 15 minutes.

Our final bit of drama was when David saw a huge black spider edging its way round to his window. Not being too fond of spiders, he tried to get rid of it as quickly as possible. Switching on the windscreen wipers he succeeded only in flipping it into his lap. Some questionable language later and a bit of acrobatics involving hanging out the open door of a moving car, and said arachnid was left behind.

It had been an eventful trip, yet we had barely touched on everything Zambia had to offer — whitewater rafting, the bird and game watching, canoeing, abseiling and horseback trails. But hey, there's always next year.

In the footsteps of crusaders

by Steve Davey

The full moon hung over the wide, flat sandy bed of the Samburu River, coating everything in an eerie soft white light and sending long shadows streaking into the undergrowth under acacia trees. The stars, normally so bold in the African sky, barely stood out against the glow of the light that showed up the footprints of the creatures that had used this parched riverbed as a thoroughfare. In the distance I heard the hoarse coughing of a prowling lion and closer, a baboon shrieked. This used to be called a bombers' moon, and quite appropriately, I was bombed.

My companions were sleeping 100m away in one of the small clearings that made up the campsite. What started as a quiet and civilised post-safari, post-dinner beer around the campfire had slowly deteriorated until only two of us were left. The last of the cold Tusker beers had been finished and it looked like the evening was over until I remembered the bottle of duty free vodka in my bag. We had been on the road solidly for the past two days and on a game drive all afternoon. I had a lot of dust to wash out of my throat, and so in an optimistically futile attempt not to disturb the others we grabbed the vodka, a couple of chairs and a clutch of mixers and walked to the middle of the dry river.

At first we were hushed, overawed by the majesty, beauty and peace of our surroundings. After a while, however, the conversation got predictably animated and garrulous. We had gone for the middle of the river bed so we could see any animals coming before they got close enough to bite, stomp or chew. A good theory, but when a cough suddenly stopped our conversation we realised that we hadn't been paying enough attention.

To my left were two Africans with rifles slung over their shoulders. They looked at us with tolerant amusement and wore the uniform of the Kenya Parks Department. They had been recruited from the local Samburu tribe and their ears were pierced and stretched into great hanging loops.

"Oh Mister, what are you doing?" demanded one of the rangers, softly lisping through a wide gap in his front teeth.

"Just having a quiet drink," I replied, trying to sound nonchalant, as if getting hammered in the middle of a game reserve was an everyday occurrence.

Their looks said it all. "Maybe you should go back to your camp, Mister," one suggested with loaded politeness, after a theatrical pause.

I hadn't been sent to bed for many years, so maybe it was my unwritten rule of always saying 'yes' to the man with the gun, or even the realisation that what we were doing was very stupid, that caused us to walk crestfallen back to the camp, crestfallen but without protest.

I'd just collapsed into my sleeping bag when there was a low call outside my tent. The rangers were back. "*Temba,*" one hissed. 'Elephant.'

I pulled on some clothes, realising just how much I'd had to drink when I tried to stuff both legs into the same hole. The rangers looked at each other and then at me with a resigned, paternal look.

They led me to the edge of the camp and pointed proudly at a large and fuzzy lump that was rustling in the undergrowth. I stared myopically into the gloom but could not make anything out. I'd taken my contact lenses out in the tent.

"Shall we go a bit closer?" I asked, only half joking.

"Oh no, very dangerous, very dangerous. It is an elephant."

I didn't have the heart to point out that it might be an elephant to them, but it was just a blurry, grey blob to me, so I stood there trying to look appreciative and not yawn.

We then set off in a crouching trot to get round to the elephant's other side. The rangers seemed to be having fun tracking through the undergrowth and were genuinely exhilarated. I just wished I could see properly.

The next morning I saw the rangers walking through the camp and offered them a cup of coffee. We talked about the park and the drought, and remembering my *mzungu*-(white-man)-meets-the-pastoralists manners, about cattle. It seemed that everything was suffering in the drought. The Samburu live to raise cattle, but seldom kill them, relying instead on a diet of milk and blood, both taken from a living animal. Because of the drought many animals had died or been slaughtered, while others had been taken to new grazing areas. This brought them into conflict with armed Somali *shifta* (bandits) and many cattle had been stolen. For the Samburu, where a man's status is gauged by the number of his cattle, it was a disaster from which it would take years to recover. The wildlife too was suffering, with many animals dying of thirst and starvation. Because of this, tourist numbers were down, and at least one lodge had closed, a blow to the local staff who worked there.

Amused by my obvious hangover, they asked me where we were heading, and when I told them Ethiopia they asked why. This is always a loaded question in Africa. There are some tribal groups, such as the Masai, who manage to maintain strong links across borders, but in general the fact that you are leaving one country to go to another can be taken as an insult. In Northern Tanzania, telling a Masai that you are going to Kenya to see what the Masai are like there will get you laughed at and told that they are the same everywhere. But it is a good answer. Trying to explain to a Kenyan the attraction of Ethiopia is a little more difficult.

I took the easy way out. I pointed to the truck, shrugged and said, "I have to go with them. What else can I do?"

They nodded sagely. It had been the right thing to say.

I couldn't adequately explain the real reason. A long time ago I'd read a confused book about the last resting place of the Ark of the Covenant. Far from being an Indiana Jones adventure, this was research that led to a church in Ethiopia's north. It hadn't been so much the story that engaged me, but the path it took to get there. My opinions of Ethiopia changed from those of one more struggling African country to a place inextricably linked with the crusaders and King Solomon's Temple. The book told of ancient monasteries hidden on islands in a lake that was the source of the Blue Nile and churches carved out of solid rock.

For most people, Ethiopian history began in the 1980s when the BBC's Michael Buerk stood in front of a suitably shocking backdrop of the starving, turned to Mohammed Amin's camera and spoke movingly of famines of biblical proportions. It sparked the furore that led to Live Aid.

Ethiopia not only has a history, it is the only African country not to be colonised — save for an ignominious defeat at the hands of the Italians — and much of that history is still there. So much of the rest of Africa only has colonial or post-colonial history left. Even Kenya only has a scattering of Swahili ruins along the coast and the Portuguese Fort Jesus in Mombasa. The rest of its tourist industry is built on the beaches and the pretence that the country has changed little since the colonial times of big game safaris where white hunters roamed the plains with spear-carrying Africans who called them *Bwana*.

My previous visits to Africa had all revolved around this standard fare of wildlife and landscapes, lightly seasoned with photogenic tribes who dressed in traditional finery and danced to order. It had been fun, but I always felt it was like some giant African Disneyland. I was looking forward to exploring a country with a real history, and one that had not been overshadowed in the great Victorian rush for space. There was also the thrill of visiting a country that had yet to be seriously touched by that other great colonising power. At the time, other than a few brief pages in its round-up of the continent, the Lonely Planet machine had yet to reach Ethiopia or bring its style of multiple-choice package tourism.

As far as missions go, this was going to be easy. I was not going to slog through rainforests or hump across deserts. I was on an overland truck from Nairobi that was to make the long drive north to Ethiopia and then pootle around for a few weeks visiting the historical sites I'd read about so long ago. This was to be a new experience for me, so it was with some trepidation that I met my fellow travellers. They had left London six months earlier and had been travelling through West and East Africa ever since. They were tired and in need of a break. To them, Ethiopia was just one more country in the mélange of memories that was their journey.

Just north of Samburu we stopped at the small town of Arthur's Post to pick up armed guards from the police station for the two day drive to the Ethiopian border. Normally they would have travelled in the back of crowded African buses and on the top of trucks, huddled with the other passengers against the dust. With his superior sitting at the front, Daniel relaxed and soon had a soda in his hand. In fact for most of the journey he seemed to be either drinking our soda or sleeping — bumping around unconsciously on the seat, the rifle between his knees bouncing off his chest. I hoped it wasn't loaded, and made sure I moved out of any potential line of fire.

The further north we got on the long bumpy ride, the more dry rivers and gaunt cattle we saw. Everywhere was parched and the fragile top soil was driven into your eyes and pores until you thought your skin would crack. It seemed inconceivable that people lived in this climate, but every few miles figures could be seen leaning into the wind and striding across the desert.

Northern Kenya was suffering from as severe a drought as parts of Ethiopia, but it was a forgotten disaster. Ethiopia is famous for being the land of famine and was receiving food aid from the West. Kenya, land of safaris, was receiving none.

Every 50 or 60km we came across a settlement of a few corrugated zinc-roofed huts and hovels made from scrubby thorn bushes. Terrible parodies of the traditional Samburu dwellings, they were built close to the town for illusory protection and supply. Most of these settlements had relatively large and recent churches built adjacent to them. The relative wealth of these modest churches mocked and dominated their humble surroundings.

Before we left our two escorts at the border and began the long drive through the Ethiopian Rift Valley to Addis Ababa, I asked Daniel if our escort was really needed. He nodded enthusiastically and told how the shifta often held up vehicles on this road. The last time had been a few months beforehand, when a dozen locals were made to lie on the ground and were then shot. The shifta come through the hills in groups of up to 40, firing off a few rounds when they see a vehicle. If fire was returned they fled back into the bush. I wondered what good two soldiers armed with old rifles would have been had 40 Somalis armed with AK47s decided to attack us. Daniel was under the happy impression that all he had to do was to fire his rifle in the air to stave off any potential attack. I changed my mind, I fervently hoped that his rifle was loaded.

I'd expected many things from Addis Ababa, but an evening rush hour traffic jam was not one of them. Neither was the rain. The three-year drought had ended, and ended in style. The menacing clouds that had been building up for the past two days and giving the daylight a malevolently metallic tinge erupted into sheets of rain. The effect was a deluge that fell from the leaden sky in a solid wall. It was like having a large bucket of water suddenly emptied over my head. One minute I was dry, the next I was reeling and looking for shelter. I was the only one. All around me faces looked up hypnotically and broke into broad grins. The rain was so heavy it muffled the laughter and shrieks of delight from the street children who minutes earlier had been sitting in the now swirling gutters looking for cash.

There seemed to be street kids everywhere. Reserved at first, when encouraged they showered you with engaging smiles and chattering conversation — hanging off arms, swinging and playing like the children they used to be. I must have looked a bizarre sight, walking around Addis Ababa with a retinue of street kids. Even the elite guard at the royal palace seemed amused.

Parts of the capital were modern and monumental, but refugees from the famine regions seemed to fill every gap. Some drove scrawny goats through the streets, thwarting the morning rush hour. Others, clad in rags and dirt, begged with doomed children and motioned hypnotically with their hands to their mouths.

It was in Addis Ababa that I realised we could not visit the historical town of Axum in the north — reputedly the home of the Ark of the Covenant itself. War had again broken out with Eritrea. Internal flights were cancelled and overland travel curtailed.

Undaunted, we set off for Bahar Dar on the shores of Lake Tana, the source of the Blue Nile. In 1770, Scotsman James Bruce discovered Lake Tana after two years of travelling. He then followed the Blue Nile until he established it as one of the sources of the river Nile itself.

Our journey only took two days, albeit two long days of hard travel across mountainous and desolate scenery. The temperature dropped with each pass we went over before we reached a flat and seemingly barren plateau where steep cliffs dropped away on either side. Even here people tried to scratch a living amongst the fierce dust clouds. They planted long rows of tall thin trees to slow down the wind that stormed though their settlements as if it were trying to sweep them over the cliff edge.

Tanks and armoured vehicles lay deserted by the side of the road. Most looked like they had just been abandoned. Some had crashed, whereas others had been wrenched apart by the force of war. These were the remnants of some past conflict, and when we stopped to inspect one of the rusting hulks the locals crowded around us, bemused that anyone would stop and take notice of what, to them, was part of the scenery.

On the shores of Lake Tana it seemed peaceful and sleepy. That was about to change. The next day was Saturday, market day, and villagers from miles around were beginning to flock to the outskirts of town.

The recent rain had left the market place looking like the Somme. I began to see why Michael Buerk had used the word 'biblical'. Not because the people were starving, just that with their sharp, dark features, white shawls and long sticks used to drive laden donkeys around they looked as if they had just stepped out of the Old Testament.

If you could ignore the mud, piles of dirt and piles of Ethiopians, the market was well organised. Each area had a section: by the side of the road was the live chicken section, then the piles of aromatic spices, then the wheat — with smiling traders flinging handfuls up in the air so it was blown away in the wind. One corner of the market was devoted to sandals made from old truck tyres. These stank badly of rubber and seemed to rely on the weight of the wearer to make them lie flat.

A young guy appeared at my shoulder and spoke earnestly in English to me. His name was Shamar and he offered to be my guide. He walked round with me, translating and easing my passage with stallholders and shoppers.

Soon a short character sidled up to us and barked a few questions — the standard name/country/destination trilogy that passes as a formal introduction when young locals are about to try to inveigle something from you. Something, probably his gold-rimmed shades, made me not like him, and we tried to get rid of him without actually telling him to bugger off. That was my weakness. I should have shaken him off there and then. He started to talk about *qat* — the herb that has been chewed in this region since before the donkey was discovered as a mode of transport. Its leaves produce a mild high and spaced inertia, but its use is spreading, leading to addiction and social problems.

Qat-boy looked like a social problem himself, but I let him lead us into a qat house — or rather a qat hovel. A wooden door opened to reveal five men sitting on narrow benches around a small gloomy room. They looked up in surprise and then, as if someone was turning down the gas, the animation in their eyes faded to a leaden stare and the life in them receded. We quickly left, and Qat-boy, hoping for a food-aid fix became petulant. Overruling my guide, he took us to a nearby qat stall.

"Buy me qat," he demanded arrogantly, grabbing a handful of leaves in a greedy narrow paw.

"Buy your own," I replied. I left suggesting beer. Shamar asked whether I wanted local or Western. I opted for local and was taken down a muddy street to a collection of huts. Qat-boy followed on his bicycle, muttering to himself.

At the beer hall I ordered a jug of beer. It was a warm, dark liquid, like homebrew served too early. The hut smelt of stale beer and staler sweat so we sat outside with the jug and some glasses. Qat-boy sat next to us and picked up a glass. I ignored him. He had taken some leaves from the stall and his eyes were already beginning to glaze over. He stared at me with open hostility. An old man hobbled over, leant on a thick stick and made the now familiar hand to mouth gesture. I motioned for him to sit down and poured him a beer in Qat-boy's still empty glass. His eyes lit up and then misted over as he focused on the glass. He cheerfully started a conversation and droned on as he drank. I had no idea what he was saying and just smiled.

The monasteries of Lake Tana are virtually hidden on small wooded islands. At sunrise the next day I boarded a small tin boat for the journey across the lake to the Kebran Gabriel monastery. A cold, damp wind was blowing and a handful of cormorants stood on rocks, wings outstretched like a crucifixion before starting the day's fishing.

After an hour in the boat huddled against the cold wind we finally reached the island. It appeared to be covered in trees except for a small beach on a narrow spit that barely reached out of the water. Leaning against the bare branch of an old tree was a monk dressed in a brown robe.

I was led up a steep path and through a stone wall that ringed the complex and into a grassy enclosure with a large circular church made of compacted mud and straw. The abbot collected an entrance fee before walking painfully over to a tall wooden door made white and brittle by age. Inside was another wall, this time decorated by rich murals. My guide translated as the abbot explained that these murals were hundreds of years old. The paints used had all been made from natural substances that never fade. The paintings showed biblical stories, often with an Ethiopian flair. Christianity came to Ethiopia in the fourth century AD, although the country also claims links through the Queen of Sheba to King Solomon and the Old Testament. Their descendent, Menelik, was the founder of the Solomon dynasty that ruled until 1974 when Emperor Haile Selassie was murdered. The 255th descendent from the House of David, Selassie is revered by followers of Rastafarianism, and the 'rasta' colours that are associated with reggae and Bob Marley are really the colours of the Ethiopian flag.

According to legend, it was Menelik who brought the Ark of the Covenant to Ethiopia from King Solomon's temple. Many of the paintings in the monasteries on Lake Tana depict this epic trip, although historians believe that if it was brought here at all it would have been 500 years later.

Inside these painted inner walls lay the holy of holies, where every Ethiopian church keeps a replica of the Ark of the Covenant, known as the *tabot*, hidden from the gaze of the faithful, yet still worshipped by them.

As I left the church the abbot turned an ornate key in a tired-looking lock. The monks on these islands have defended the treasures of their religion for centuries, sometimes even with their lives. It is believed the Ark was brought to this monastery and hidden for 800 years. In a small outlying building the abbot displayed the relics, including an ornate cross and a silver crown from the ruler of a long forgotten kingdom. Perhaps the greatest treasure was an illustrated manuscript of the four gospels dating back to the 14th century. It had pages made of treated goatskin and was expansively illuminated in the same bold colours as the church walls. It was so vivid that it looked like it had just been painted.

In contrast to the monasteries, whose mud walls and bright colours belie their real age, the carved churches of Lalibala — a day's long and bumpy drive to the east — have an intensely medieval feel. They were constructed in the seventh century on a 2,600m-high rock terrace. Nothing prepares you for their grandeur and complexity — certainly not the town, which is typically run-down. The churches are beautiful in style and proportion. They are arranged in three groups, the most famous of which is Beta Ghiorghis — St George's church — which is carved into the solid red rock. From above it takes the shape of a cross, one of the reasons why some have attributed the building of the churches to the crusaders who are thought to have brought the Ark of the Covenant from the Holy Land.

The heat and light from outside failed to penetrate the church's dark recesses and a cool sense of order and contemplation prevailed. A dome rises above the sanctuary and a crusaders' double-barred cross decorates the interior. Ornate drapes on the walls masked some of the finer detail, but it was still possible to see the craftsmanship that went into the construction.

Approaching the Beta Mariam group of churches, I heard the sounds of drums echoing through the entrance tunnel. Like Beta Ghiorghis, this building was set in a deep pit. The mischievous faces of children peered over the edge at the devotions going on below. A group of priests were holding a special mass in the shady confines of the courtyard. Carpets had been laid on the floor for them to sit on and a patterned red cloth hung on the wall behind them. The priests wore white turbans and each held a long thin walking stick with a silver top. Large umbrellas fringed with gold brocade were held above them as they chanted from an enormous Bible.

Inside the church it was chaos. Some people knelt around praying, while others pushed their way to the front to kiss an ornate cross held by a priest. A brightly coloured painting of the Madonna and Child was partially covered out of respect. One old woman with deep lines etched into her dark brown face kissed the cross, then prostrated herself near-hysterically in front of the picture.

Christianity in Ethiopia was different from what I had seen elsewhere in Africa, having been adopted and developed by the people in antiquity and not thrust upon them by missionaries. In this way it is an integral part of the Ethiopian national character, not a heritage left behind by colonisation.

The long journey back to Addis Ababa took us over some of the highest inhabited passes in the country. It was so cold people were swaddled in blankets, woolly hats and warm clothes during the day. Everything was dry and unproductive, and there seemed to be little difference between cultivated and uncultivated land. Every so often we passed lorries loaded with sacks of flour. Although the rain had come, people still needed aid while they waited for their crops to grow.

One village we passed had a feeding programme in town. Villagers were driving donkeys loaded with grain sacks against us, and as we tried to drive through, they just smiled and waved. The sacks were stamped with the logo of the European Union and they linked us inextricably with that aid.

This was the message that was being carried by the media to the outside world: a starving Ethiopia, not a country whose culture has roots going back to the Old Testament. A country of suffering, not a land where rulers traced their lineage back to King Solomon, where Rastafarianism began and the land that was possibly the last resting place of the Ark of the Covenant. Ethiopia might have a history, but no one seemed interested it it, preferring instead latching onto famine, drought and warfare.

Passing through this oppressive landscape it occurred to me that we were doing nothing to help the Ethiopians by classing them as victims, rather than people with a long and noble history. Giving them a proper future would take more than conscience-salving food aid.

Canoeing on the Zambezi

by Graham Boynton

W e were standing on the banks of the Ume River just a hundred metres from where it feeds into Lake Kariba. Dawn had broken, and white-crowned plovers were switching and swirling overhead, squawking out warnings to the animals below that there were bipeds afoot.

Spike Williamson, our guide, was studying the spoor on the veld track. Waterbuck had passed this way recently, as had two elephants, some hyenas, and a troop of baboons. There was something missing. "We don't see rhino spoor here anymore," said Spike. "The last time was about a year ago. They'd been poached out."

It had been some years since I last stood on the same spot with Spike, but I remembered finding rhino spoor easily and then trekking off after these magnificent beasts knowing we would find them. It wasn't too long ago that Zimbabwe's conservationists reckoned they had between 1,500 and 2,500 black rhino in the Zambezi Valley — the largest population left in wild Africa. Now almost 90% have been poached, and the remaining few have been relocated onto private lands. There may be one or two isolated individuals out there somewhere, but nowadays the only rhino you see are the bloody, butchered carcasses. Most of the poachers come across the Zambezi from neighbouring Zambia, and the vastness of the terrain and the limited resources of Zimbabwe's anti-poaching units have conspired with these armed peasants and their fat-cat masters to render the valley's rhino extinct.

When Spike takes bush walks around the shores of Lake Kariba these days, he finds himself reminiscing. About how in late 1990 he'd seen a large male rhino under that tree. And how the following year, just beyond that ridge, he managed to get within 15m of a female and her calf. As he led our group up from the shore and across the brow of a hill toward a small herd of feeding elephants, Spike offered a grave warning. "Now that the rhino are finished," he said, "the poachers will turn on the elephants. In fact, they've already started." We stood silent and still for a while, not 20m from a large single-tusked bull as it tore up clumps of grass with its trunk, beat the sand out against its leg, and then chewed it to a pulp, all the time keeping a watchful eye on us.

In the silence Spike's words ran through my head. Then the big bull suddenly reared its head and turned to face us. Clearly one of our party had made a sudden movement and we'd become a threat. He flapped his ears, stamped the ground, and charged. Spike stood quite still and waved his arms, shouting "Bugger off! Bugger off!" With ten metres to go, the big bull stormed off to the right and away into the bush. The adrenalin in our veins had swept aside thoughts of Africa's wildlife crisis. This was what we had come to the Zambezi for. This was wild Africa at its most exhilarating.

We had met in Harare, Zimbabwe's capital, two days earlier. Our group comprised an English stock-broker who had grown up in Africa; a Johannesburg advertising executive who spent much of his time off in the bush; an Australian nurse; the photographer Håkan Ludwigsson and tropical medicine expert Dr Richard Dawood. The plan was to fly to the shores of Lake Kariba and spend a couple of days at a floating camp called Water Wilderness before taking to canoes and making our way along the Zambezi River to Chikwenya Camp, on the edge of the Mana Pools National Park. This is the Middle Zambezi Valley, one of the most remote and underpopulated wildlife outposts on the continent. Although the black rhino is all but gone, the valley is still abundant with animals and birdlife.

Harare is no longer the dreamy miniature city I remember from my youth. Since independence in 1980, it has become one of the world's choice foreign posts and is awash with embassies, consulates, foreign aid organisations, consultants, advisers, study groups, and every other concerned Western facilitator you care to think of. In the city centre there are traffic jams of shiny designer 4WDs and late-model Mercedes, the former favoured by the aid-agency, rural-development, and wildlife-conservancy people, the latter by the diplomats and politicos. It has been said that there are more Mercedes per licensed driver in Harare than in any other world capital.

We scrounged around the city for a day, gathering up items like torches, knives, rope, khaki shirts, and a package of outstanding maps — another legacy of the colonials — from the government cartography office. The second night we toasted our safari with a bottle of dreadful Zimbabwean wine and agreed that we had seen enough of Harare.

A 90-minute hop in a Queenair plane took us from Harare to Bumi Hills on the shores of Lake Kariba. I was relieved that Spike was there to meet us. A cheerful, easy-going young man in his mid-20s, he is one of the most erudite guides in the country and knows the flora and fauna of this part of the Zambezi better than anyone. He has been the guide-in-residence at Water Wilderness for the past five years and was marvellous company on my last trip out here. Since then I had heard that he was planning to move to Botswana or join his brother's Ivory Lodge operation at Hwange National Park, but he still seemed unable to tear himself away from this unique environment.

As we waited around Bumi Hills while Spike finalised provisions and arrangements for our stay at Water Wilderness, we began to understand why he was so reluctant to leave. The hotel itself is a motel-like arrangement of neat and perfectly clean bungalows; its location, however, must be among the planet's top ten. It is perched on one of three hills overlooking the southern shore of Lake Kariba, with Zambia across the water to the north and the Matusadona National Park off in the distance to the east. From our vantage point the elephants on the shore were mere dots on a massive canvas, and the hippos wading in the water looked like fleas. Kariba is one of the largest man-made lakes in the world — 120km long and 32km across at its widest. It was formed with the completion of Kariba Dam in 1958 and caused massive disruption to the human and animal populations. Thirty years later both have adapted to a new eco-system — as all species must do if they are to survive.

Water Wilderness is a collection of five wooden houseboats moored in an estuary a half hour's boat ride from the Bumi Hills. At dawn and dusk, when the sun plays on the water and the petrifying forest of half-submerged trees surrounding the houseboats, it is like nowhere else on earth. You assemble, eat, drink, and organise on the mother boat, and then at evening's end, after a few bottles of wine, you stumble into the canoes and paddle off to a floating bedroom somewhere out in the inky night. On the first evening this was a sobering experience as the deep, resonant grunting of the hippos bounced across the water, and with each stroke of the paddle I expected a giant shape to rear out of the water and upend us.

At Water Wilderness we received our first briefing on how to deal with hippos while travelling in fragile, fibreglass canoes at no more than ten kilometres an hour. The Zambezi is full of hippos that gather in colonies, or pods, of up to 50. They are among Africa's most dangerous wild animals and are responsible for many deaths each year. "It's simple," said Spike. "Never get your canoe between the hippos and their routes of escape to the deep water." And if you found yourself inadvertently in that position? "Then there's a chance he'll have a nip at you," he said with a smile.

Of course, nip is hardly what hippos do. Armed with large tusks and powerful jaws, they present a most fearsome sight when they explode out of the water. When, on a recent safari here two America fishermen invited their African chef to join them on an evening boat ride, a look of alarm spread over his face. "You must think I'm crazy," he cried. "There are animals in that water with mouths like open suitcases."

On day three we said goodbye to Spike and flew off to join our canoes and new guide at Vundu camp, a cluster of tents set up for us ten kilometres downstream from the Ruckomechi River mouth. Mike Pelham picked us up at the Mana Pools airstrip, and as we bumped across the rutted track toward the camp, he said he wanted to make a detour to check on the condition of an ailing lioness. Within five minutes we pulled the Land Rover over on a patch of open veld, and there was the lioness standing quite still. It was a poignant sight. She was on the verge of death, an emaciated skeleton unable to move but seemingly determined not to lie down and die quite yet. Vulture hovered overhead and hyenas would probably rip her apart that night. Someone asked whey she wasn't shot and put out of her misery, and Mike said that National Parks policy was to interfere as little as possible and to let nature take its course. It is clearly the right policy; still, we drove away from the once-proud creature feeling uneasy. (We later learned that soon after, a park warden had taken pity and shot her.)

Before we took to our canoes, we were given the full briefing on the sweet science of canoeing down the Zambezi. Mike repeated Spike's warning about getting between a hippo and its route of escape, and then explained what to do if we were charged and banged out of the canoe. The first thing is to hang onto the upturned canoe, and next is to remember not to dangle your legs in the water, since that is an invitation for the crocodiles to move in. He told us that in two-and-a-half years as a canoe guide he hadn't lost a client, and, thus reassured, we took to the water, a little shakily at first, but with some authority as the day passed.

It would be dishonest to suggest that we were emulating the great Victorian explorers and adventurers, such as David Livingstone and Frederick Courtney Selous, who first alerted the world to this wild Eden. A quick perusal of Selous' diary of his expedition along the Zambezi in 1878 reveals the sheer bravery and single-mindedness of these men in the face of incredible hardship. Selous, his companion LM Owen and many of the bearers and guides came down with '*the fever*' (presumably blackwater fever), Owen so seriously that he lost the use of his limbs. By January 11th, Selous writes, they were all down with '*fever of a very virulent form, and in the depths of a starving country. Eight wretched little Kafir fowls, about the size of a bantam ... and a little Kafir corn ... was all we had to eat and drink.*'

They soldiered on for several weeks, with Owen carried on a litter and Selous struggling along weakly. They covered little more than eight kilometres a day, through thick bush under an overpowering summer sun. The mosquitoes kept them awake at night, their bearers were constantly on the verge of revolt, and Selous was too weak to hunt. On February 29th Selous shot a zebra and they ate. Finally, he decided to leave Owen with his Basuto servant and strike out for help in Matabele country, '*ten days' hard walking for a healthy Kafir, across a very rough, broken country.*' He arrived at Inyati, '*exhausted in body, but joyful in mind,*' almost three weeks later. Owen was duly rescued and Selous spent the next few months recuperating in Gubulawayo before heading straight back in August to his beloved bushveld.

Although we were travelling in Selous' footsteps, we were hardly sharing his experiences. While he was taking on a raw, unchartered wilderness teeming with wild animals and rife with terrible diseases, we were drifting through the valley on a highly organised luxury safari, with excellent meals prepared for us morning and night, iceboxes filled with Castle lager to sip on when we broke sweat, and very little danger of being killed by wild animals. Besides, we had the irrepressibly health-conscious Dr Dawood monitoring our every ailment and providing a pharmaceutical *cordon sanitaire* between ourselves and raw nature. Armed as he was with enough surgical equipment in his hand luggage to perform minor transplants, we all agreed that Dr Dawood was a necessary addition to any safari.

With the folds of the Zambian escarpment on our left and the dense woodland of Mana Pools on our right, we canoed past pod after pod of hippos, passing groups of elephants swimming from the mainland to the islands to feed on the torpedo grass, suddenly finding goliath herons lifting out of the reeds just a few feet from the canoes. The only noises were of the oars splashing in the water, the metallic, tinkling call of the blacksmith plovers, and the resonant booms across the water from the hippo pods. It was if we were tiptoeing through an ancient world that modern man had overlooked.

This section of the Zambezi River meanders through an 8,000-square-kilometre valley floor between two gorges — the Kariba Gorge upstream and the Mupata Gorge 200km downstream at the Mozambique border. The valley floor consists of a series of terraces, each with its own distinct soil type and vegetation, running from the banks of the river to the foot of the escarpment. Near the river the torpedo grass, ilala palms and sausage trees give way first to grassy plain and Acacia albida and Natal mahogany, then to the jesse bushveld that is so dense you could hide a fleet of pink Cadillacs in it. During the heavy summer rains — November to February — animals leave the river and head into the jesse, to return again during the dry winter months in search of water.

This cycle continued uninterrupted for as long as it did because the valley was protected from settlement by humans and domestic livestock by a fly. The dreaded tsetse causes sleeping sickness in humans, and *nagana*, a fatal disease, in livestock, so until eradication programmes were introduced in the 1960s, the area wasn't fit for human habitation. Hand in hand with this pharmaceutical progress has come the increasing demand for land from a rapidly growing population, a problem endemic to modern Africa. As we canoed along the river, we saw no outsiders for days on end, so it was difficult to imagine this place overrun with people. But in 50 years' time it will be equally hard to imagine any corner of the continent being devoid of human beings.

Early on our second morning on the river we were again reminded of the more immediate problem of the missing black rhino population. We had been canoeing for a couple of hours when Mike gave the signal to pull into shore for breakfast. After securing our canoes, we took a short walk through the bush, and Mike pointed out the proliferation of fever-berry croton, a favourite food of black rhinos. "In the short time since the rhino has disappeared," he told us, "the croton has flourished, creating an imbalance in the ecosystem that may have serious consequences." And then he pointed to the spot where he last saw a black rhino more than a year ago. "I sometimes look at the ground and see something resembling rhino spoor," he said quietly. "I try to convince myself that it is a rhino print … but, of course, it isn't. They're gone."

Zimbabwe conservationists admit they have been routed by the rhino poachers. In the mid-80s the population was the largest in Africa, almost all of it concentrated here in the Zambezi Valley. But as the decade drew to a close and the money the government allocated to national parks dwindled, Zimbabwe began losing up to 200 a year. This year the national parks ran out of money at the end of the first quarter and since then have been existing on hand-outs, largely from the private sector.

Zimbabwe was once envied by the rest of Africa for its wildlife programmes and its conservationists. While East Africa was being ravaged by ivory and rhino-horn poaching, Zimbabwe seemed in control, containing poaching with a no-nonsense strong-arm policy and creating conservation programmes that were forward-thinking models for post-colonial Africa. For example, the much copied CAMPFIRE communal conservation schemes give wildlife a financial value and thus provide incentives for rural people to protect the animals. Although many of the programmes are still in place and some of the experienced conservationists are still operating, the country's wildlife agenda seems in jeopardy. The virtual extinction of the black rhino is surely a deafening and early warning.

When I last saw Zimbabwe's leading conservation scientist, Rowan Martin, he described how well rhino relocation and captive breeding programmes had been going. Then he paused and said slowly: "But we have fallen down badly on the conservation of large wild populations. For a long time I have been making the point that it is not a case of 'Chaps, do the best you can with a poor budget.' It is an absolute threshold condition.

Below a certain budget you fail. I feel great sadness... because I suppose we've cocked it up. They've gone."

By the sixth day we had our routines down pat: rise before dawn, grab a cup of coffee, and head off into the bush for a tow-hour hike. We would go looking for the lion pride we had heard roaring the previous night, track down an elephant herd we knew was in the area, or follow the hyena spoor from just outside our tents through the cluster of Natal mahogany trees into the thick jesse bush.

By 9am we would be back in camp and tucking into a hearty breakfast. Having eaten — and thought guiltily about Selous and his eight wretched *'little Kafir fowls'* — we would climb into the canoes and continue the journey east. As the day wore on and the sun began to drop behind the Zambian escarpment, we would allow the canoes to drift with the current and silently thread their way through shallow inlets adorned with lilac-breasted rollers, egrets, black-winged stilts, water dikkops, white-fronted bee-eaters, saddle-bill storks, marabou storks. By sunset we were usually at our tented camp for the night or on the water near it.

But on that sixth day, the day we thought we had it down pat, we had our first major confrontation with our surroundings. We had been canoeing for an hour when we arrived at a promontory that required careful negotiation — a large hippo was lurking no more that 15m offshore and was looking most threatening. As the lead canoe, containing Dr Dawood and Mike Pelham, rounded the corner, the hippos moved toward it, and Mike grabbed at some foliage to keep the canoe up against the shore. The tuft came away in his hand, and suddenly the current swept the front of the canoe across the face of the hippo. Dr Dawood's extended legs passing no more than a few feet from the animal. In an instant their canoe was out of the range, and the hippo turned its attention to the rest of us. We managed to inch past it without incident, but at dinner that night, Mike, an understated fellow, admitted it had been a close call.

Not an hour later we were adding to our trophy cupboard of stories, following a small group of elephants across one of the wider and deeper sections of the river. The problem wasn't the elephants, which barely noticed these flea-like attendants, but more hippos, which we careered past in the deep middle channel, not seeing them until the last minute. Sometimes manoeuvring a canoe is like running in quicksand, and so it was that day. We were out in the fast-flowing open river, paddling like hell, digging deep into the water and pulling back with every muscle, and still we were drifting inexorably toward the mouth of one of the hippos. A final surge of adrenalin and we got past, and I suppose in retrospect it wasn't really that close. But the moment left us with a strong sense of how puny we were, how impotent in the hands of nature.

Our arrival at Chikwenya Camp, where we were to spend the last two nights of our safari, was marked by our first sighting of the 'chewed canoe'. It belonged to a group travelling a day behind us and had sunk when an angry hippo charged it and bit a large chunk out of the side. The occupants escaped unharmed, but the beast's tusks missed the legs of the fellow at the front by a whisker. As we stared at the broken boat, we wondered whether it had been the same hippo that almost took a nip at Dr Dawood. Then we puffed ourselves up a bit, because at last we had found material evidence of the lurking dangers we had been negotiating our way through for the past five days.

Such foolish pride is soon extinguished in Africa, as we found out that night around the campfire at Chikwenya. Just as the wine flowed, so did the fearful stories. Our own exaggerated near-encounters were quickly eclipsed by tales of three serious hippo attacks last year, one of which resulted in a man's death. And only a week earlier a foreign aid worker had been hunted down by a bull elephant in a mealie field and trampled to death as he cowered behind a termite mound.

The stories have an added poignancy at Chikwenya, a camp founded in 1982 and run by admired naturalist, hunter and guide, John Stevens. He had been there for only nine months when his three-year-old daughter, Briarley, was attacked by a lioness in the camp. The child's spinal cord was severed and she is now confined to a wheelchair. After that, Stevens left Chikwenya, and fellow naturalist Jeff Stutchbury, who had started up Water Wilderness in the late 70s, took over in 1984. It was Stutchbury's widow, Veronica, who was running it during our visit.

For all these violent encounters with wild animals, you may be safer in the bush than in midtown Manhattan on a Saturday night. Every year a few thousand tourists thread their way through the wilderness, and attacks on them are rare. But there is nothing like sitting ten centimetres above the waterline in a fibreglass shell facing two tons of hippopotamus with a mouth like an open suitcase to fully appreciate the impotence of a floating, two-metre long, 90-kilogram version of *homo sapiens*.

Chikwenya also provided us with our first encounter with outsiders for five days and it took a little getting used to. Dr Dawood, however, relished the infusion of new blood (as it were), for among the camp staff, the camp pilot, the game guides, and the visiting locals were many victims of malaria. This is one of our tropical disease detective's special subjects, an every evening he could be found hovering around the campfire like and anopheles mosquito, waiting to alight on anyone with a good malaria story to tell. Mike Pelham had a very good one. He had had malaria five times in the past 30 months, each episode progressively worse than the last. It's just one of the occupational hazards of working in the bush.

Dr Dawood was astonished that, like most of the Zimbabweans he had met, Mike was blasé about a disease that is now among the biggest killers on the African continent. As he had done on our previous safaris together, the good doctor equipped us with coils, pills, sprays, and nets that no mosquito managed to penetrate in ten days.

On our final night, we sat around the campfire at Chikwenya and toasted Mike Pelham, then toasted the Zambezi River, then Africa. Just as we seemed to have adjusted to the rhythm of this place, acclimatised ourselves to the subtlety of sounds and movements, it was time to re-enter the real world. The London stockbroker had brought along Jurassic Park to read on the safari and had only managed to get to page ten. We hadbeen out here for eight days, and they had come and gone in the flicker of an eye.

Before we left, Dr Dawood gave Mike one of the permethrin-impregnated mosquito nets. Mike was chuffed and announced that Dawood had convinced him to renounce the old ways and to protect himself against malaria. As we flew out and circled over the Zambezi Valley, we all agreed we should do it again. We should.

Since Graham Boynton's journey, Zimbabwe has been in the grip of a serious political and social crisis. His broad observations about conservation politics, however, remain true.

Routes of the family tree

by Chris Bradley

The last time I saw my mother's uncle Jim was at my grandfather's funeral in Bolton. I was 19 and just starting out in life. He was 70 and just finishing. After the Second World War, disillusioned with victory, rationing and the poor quality of life, he hitch-hiked across Africa before settling in South Africa and then Rhodesia, as Zimbabwe was then known in 1948. I'd been nowhere and his life sounded incredibly adventurous. If wanderlust is a contagious disease, then I caught it from him.

When Italy declared war against Britain in June 1940, they had 300,000 troops ready to advance from Cyrenaica in Eastern Libya towards the British soldiers defending Egypt and the Suez Canal. Jim, then aged 38, was evacuated from Dunkirk and would soon be sent to join the North African Campaign.

Tripoli, capital of the newly opened Libya, is an easy-going place, where everyone seems to have plenty of time to sit in large light piazzas drinking small dark coffees. Imagine a combination of the waterfront of Casablanca, the narrow streets of Alexandria, with a bit of rebuilt Beirut thrown in and you pretty much have it. Around every corner are portraits of Colonel Gaddafi. Huge paintings showed him at the helm of the giant oil tanker that is Libya, negotiating the shark-infested waters of international politics. In most of the poses he is looking dramatically into the far distance, as if trying to see what's coming over the next hill.

I'd been surprised by his apparent about-turn on Arab matters. As self-proclaimed successor to Egypt's Nasser, Gaddafi now seems no longer interested in the Middle East, and is looking south towards Africa. All the propaganda posters now show Libya as the guiding light for African unity — surely an even greater oxymoron than Arab unity.

I wasn't exactly following in Jim's footsteps, but I was curious to see a place that he'd known, albeit in very different circumstances. The idea of visiting Libya and just sticking to the coastal theatres of war was never an option. On earlier Saharan visits to Djanet and Tam in southern Algeria, and even as far south as Timbuktu in Mali, I'd heard of the fabled desert town of Ghadhames. For thousands of years it controlled the northern edge of the trans-Saharan trade, supplying exotic goods to Europe. Trade from the remote regions of Mali, Niger and the Sahel included ivory, gold and slaves. Even the wild animals used in gladiatorial battles were transported through here, and so important was this trade that the Romans built a desert fortress guarding the main route into Ghadhames — the furthest south the Roman Empire ever stretched.

Tripolitania was the bustling *entrepôt* of Saharan trade. The desert through which tradesmen struggled was a dangerous adversary, but it was also their protector. Who, other than the Tuareg, could even think of making a home, let alone a living, in the middle of the Sahara? But these are not romantic views of simple trade routes. Crossing the Sahara on foot has never been easy, and even for the local caravan traders, four or five crossings were considered a lifetime's achievement.

I hired a small, wizened Berber driver by the name of Mohammed. Heading south from Tripoli we passed through the large town of al-Aziziyah, an unremarkable place but for its appearance in millions of copies of the *Guinness Book of Records*. Until recently, the world's highest temperature in the shade was recorded here at 58°C on September 13, 1922. Apparently a place in Eritrea has since beaten that. The Italians sure chose the best places to colonise.

It wasn't quite that hot today, but with the windows down it was still like having fan heaters blowing in. We pulled into a government-owned petrol station where Mohammed filled up for less than £2. I explained that in the UK such an amount was less than the allowable minimum. I also told him about the 'Dump the Pump' phenomenon, which he took as a typical British attack on Arab oil producers. He mistrusted me from then on, even when I told him that we paid 25 times more than him for fuel.

African driving is a bit like its music. It appears well ordered with a natural flow and rhythm, especially when beefed up by modern Asian or Western technology. But you know that at any moment the tempo can rise and an improvised solo performance can suddenly be unleashed. Mohammed's tempo always seemed a bit on the high side. Unlike him, I fitted my seatbelt.

The driver of a slower car in front flopped an arm out of the window. An almost imperceptible twitch of his index finger could have meant any or all of three things:

(1) He was about to turn left

(2) He acknowledged Mohammed's continual flashing of headlights and wished to enter into a discussion about the size of his manhood (road rage Libyan style)

(3) His entire body suffered from nervous twitches and he was liable to suddenly veer violently from side to side of the road for no apparent reason. Fortunately it was the first, leaving someone else to worry about the possibility of it being one of the others.

The route took us over the Nafusa Mountains, about 100km inland, and ran parallel to the coast. An important supplier of foodstuffs over the millennia, these rolling hills behind the escarpment have always been Berber strongholds. Some of the strangest features are the fortified granaries in many of the older villages. At Nalut, the granary is perched on the edge of a 500m-high cliff in an abandoned section of the old town.

These strange circular storage compounds made from mud and stone also double as refuges for the villagers during attacks. Hundreds of narrow chambers are stacked one above the other, four storeys high, with walled sections for different grains and huge embedded olive oil pots and tiny wooden doors. It looked like a civil engineer had been asked to build an advent calendar.

Beyond Nalut the Sahara starts. First as vast stretches of scrubland, then distant sand dunes interrupting the flat horizon. The route is almost due south, and the further we drove the more the dunes encroached on the road. The scale of the landscape and the absence of traffic lulls both driver and passenger into a trance, where distances of metres become kilometres

— and vice versa. Suddenly the car pitched and lurched as it hurdled a ridge of sand running across the tarmac and ploughed uncontrollably into the side of another. We both cracked our heads on the roof and I'm not sure whether the scream came from me or Mohammed, but a faceful of sand through the open window cut it short.

Wedged against the small dune, Mohammed's door refused to budge. Spitting grains of sand, I got out and surveyed our snakelike tyre tracks. We had bounced over the first two ridges and used the third as a ramp to dive into the larger fourth dune. Two metres to the left and we would have missed them completely. Mohammed struggled out of my door and inspected the crumpled wheel arch. We pushed the car clear and it started OK. From then on, thankfully, he reduced his speed, helped by a wheezing noise coming from somewhere underneath.

Arriving in Ghadhames, I realised that the distance we had covered in one day took the Scottish explorer Gordon Laing two months to complete in 1826. His 13-month trek across the Sahara from Tripoli, to become the first white man into Timbuktu, is one of the greatest feats of endurance of all time. He died on the return trip, never to consummate his marriage to Emma, the beautiful daughter of the British Consul in Tripoli. His painfully slow progress was relayed back to her by the use of the desert postal system. The hooks for the mailbags still hang in the dusty old town, little changed since Laing's time.

Guidebooks, especially those aimed at the less than adventurous visitor, often describe a souk or an old town as easy to get lost in. But this place actually lives up to that description and is like nowhere that I have ever seen. Split into tribal sections between the local ethnic groups, it is a labyrinth of square subways. They seem to be underground until you suddenly tumble out of a side door at ground level and into the glare of a small garden or date plantation.

The site was originally chosen because of the water supply from the Ain al-Faras, the 'Spring of the Mare'. In such an arid place, water is the key to life and a valuable commodity to be strictly regulated by a respected local elder, known as the *Na'ib*. Even as late as the 1950s, each farmer paid for his supply, controlled not by volume, but by time. A bucket filled by the Na'ib from the channel leaked water through a small hole, emptying after about three minutes, a unit of time known as a *qadoos*. Each time the bucket emptied, a knot was tied in a palm frond to monitor the amount sent to that farmer. Nine qadoos was equal to a *dermaysa*. The farmers were allowed to irrigate for so many knots, or more importantly, were told to get workers ready for redirecting water to their fields when it became their turn.

The government has provided new houses for many Libyans, especially those in remote areas who need greater help to join the 21st century. Gaddafi is proud of his family's traditional desert roots and sees the plight of the rural and semi-nomadic communities as a priority. Gaddafi the Tuareg appears on giant paintings, wrapped completely in billowing indigo clothing.

The new town overlooks the old, which is not quite abandoned. The houses of the old town are still maintained, the locals clinging to their culture in the face of rapid development. Each house is a maze of small rooms and passages, decorated in traditional red paint, mirrors and pots.

In summer, the men still prefer their old haunts and wander down to the cool, shady corners for a chat, rather than suffer in the heat of the newer houses. But by sunset almost all have gone, leaving the dusty tunnels to the silent swoops of bats and the distant call of the muezzin. As each bat swung across a bright entranceway, its body would become a floating X-ray as its skeleton curved this way and that before disappearing into the gloom once more. This is the time when the ghosts of 1,000 years emerge from the shadows. Muted voices and soft footfalls echoed along the twisting corridors from who knows where. As the dust settled from another scorching day, shafts of light and shade played tricks in the fading dusk.

Ghadhames lies at what is now the meeting point of the borders of Libya, Algeria and Tunisia. But today's trans-Saharan traffic into Libya is negligible, given the strict control each country places on the import and export of goods (both legal and otherwise). The Tuareg, once the master mariners and pirates of the sand seas with their caravans of hundreds of beasts, are now reduced to taking the (very) occasional tourist on 4WD sunset tea-runs across the dunes just outside town. The man at the town museum told me he had only seen four small groups of British visitors in the last 12 months.

Each country with a Tuareg presence is keen to limit their movements with inducements of schools, clinics, jobs and passports. There has long been talk of an independent Tuareg state, but even this is anathema to people who for centuries have wandered freely, wherever they choose. Only the introduction of artificial lines on maps that has fuelled such moves.

Distances across Libya are huge. From the Algerian border to Tobruk is about 1800km, a stretch similar to the distance between Monaco and Athens along the north Mediterranean coast. Mohammed and I struck obliquely for the coast and headed for Al-Khums, the town nearest to what are arguably the greatest Roman ruins in the world.

Leptis Magna is huge and I had it to myself. The Severan forum and nearby basilica are on such a massive, decorative scale that it's almost impossible to imagine them complete. Italian archaeologists are in the process of repairing and rebuilding, but I reckon they've still got another millennium to go.

For me the real gem is out to the east, beyond the silted harbour, to the circus and the amphitheatre, two of the truly great monumental buildings of Roman North Africa. Sitting alone on the upper tier of the amphitheatre, with the turquoise sea rolling in behind, you can just imagine Russell Crowe, battling it out in the centre.

In early 1941, British troops pushed the Italians back across Cyrenaica and beyond Benghazi. They could have continued on to Tripoli had the supply of troops to Greece not been of greater overall priority.

It is 900km to Benghazi from Leptis, along the busy coastal road around the Gulf of Sirt. This sounds pleasant, but for most of the time the road is kilometres inland and the only views across flat scrub are of a million shredded tyres and dumped rubbish, framed by distant electricity pylons.

Beyond Sirt, it was not difficult to spot a giant pipe section of the Great Man-Made River Project. Altogether there is about 4,000km of pipeline, some four metres in diameter, to channel plentiful underground water from the desert to urban coastal centres. Nearby, a giant poster shows Gaddafi the engineer, complete with hard hat.

At a place called Sultan there is a strange little museum. Stretched out on the ground in a compound set back from the highway are two giant bronze statues of naked men looking like they might be posing for *Playgirl's* nude 'action goalkeeper of the month'. In the 6th century, a unique, if impractical solution to settling territorial disputes was chosen. In order to set a frontier between Carthage to the west and Cyrenaica in the east, two pairs of runners set out from each capital. Wherever they met would be the border.

A look at the map shows that the Philaeni brothers, running from the west, covered a huge distance compared to the runners from Cyrenaica.

The brothers were accused of cheating, and in their keenness to swear their honesty, offered to be buried alive at the spot. Buried they were, and it fell to Mussolini to re-erect a monument in their honour in the 1930s. The giant sprawling figures and a few broken slabs are all that remain of the Philaeni's Marble Arch.

Huge oil refineries at Bin Jawwad, Ras Lannuf and Aqaylah now dominate the coast. It was also the start of my personal quest, as Aqaylah was the furthest place west taken by the British as they pursued the retreating Italians.

Hitler's response came in the guise of Erwin Rommel, commander of the Afrika Corps. Throughout 1941 he used brilliant military tactics and manoeuvres to push the Allied forces back beyond Ajdabiya, Benghazi and towards the Ghazala line.

Benghazi has a very pleasant feel to it, especially downtown Benghazi. With no idea of what to expect, it reminded me a bit of Vancouver or parts of urban Florida with its large stretches of inland lakes surrounded by parks and recreation areas. But that distant view is just about where the similarity ends. Bombed to pieces and retaken by both sides during the war, little remains of the old town, separated from the new urban sprawl by flyovers and arterial roads.

A charming cultural throwback is the horse-drawn *caleche*, but it now seems out of place when everyone appears to have a car. A common sight in Upper Egypt, here they ply their trade at the side of the sports stadium overlooking the romantically named 23rd July Lake. Local visitors to the big city then get taken on a ten-minute tour, which takes the horses away from the stadium and onto a motorway slip road. They then battle with trucks leaving the port, to merge with traffic on the flyover and clip-cloppingly negotiate a large roundabout before swinging back to the waterfront — and all of this on tarmac, amid blaring horns and flashing headlights. It is even more bizarre at night when the caleches are fitted with car lights.

That evening I ate outside at a pizzeria near the lake. At first I took the shouting match between two waiters to be light-hearted banter, but it developed into a scuffle and suddenly became a fight. Each had their supporters amongst the other staff and at one point I was caught between a knife-wielding shawarma man and the pizza oven chef rolling up his sleeves. It didn't seem the right time to ask about extra olives.

After peace had resumed I walked back around the lake and stopped to inspect a car very similar to my own 11-year old white Vauxhall Astra. This one was owned by Khaled, a boy racer. He was surrounded by loads of mates all sat on their bonnets, listening to Arabic music or fiddling with the cars' electrics.

"What else can we do?" he said in Arabic, shrugging. "I need money, to get a wife, to get a life. Here there's nothing happening."

Like a lot of people in and around Benghazi he worked in the oil industry. But it was office work that paid poorly and he was stuck. In fact, people all over Libya seem to be waiting for something to happen, or trying to get out. Everyone seems to be in a type of limbo.

The drive from Benghazi took me into the Jebel Akhdar, the 'Green Mountains' of Cyrenaica. The dusty red sheep and vast open stretches reminded me of Tuscany or Sicily — no wonder the Italians felt at home here. This independent area was controlled directly from Rome, with immigrants given land and homes in the 1920s so they could establish dominance. Many of these yellowing Italian villas still stand, but in an ironic twist, they are now used as cattle sheds or barns beside newer Libyan houses with air-conditioning and ensuites.

The site of old Cyrene is Libya's version of Delphi — a classical Greek city tumbling down a hillside. And like Leptis, you can have the whole place to yourself. It was close to here that one of the most daring escapades of the war took place.

Some of the most astonishing war adventures came from a band of almost totally independent soldiers known as the Long Range Desert Group. Nominally based in British-held oases in Egypt's Western Desert and even as far south as Sudan, they made daring raids on enemy positions after incredible Saharan journeys of thousands of kilometres. Aided by the fledgling SAS they attacked airfields, bases and depots way behind enemy lines before melting back into the desert.

The opening scene of the *The Desert Fox* depicted one of the most audacious operations by the LRDG — the planned assassination of Rommel at his commandeered villa HQ near to Cyrene. The group succeeded in attacking and entering the building, but lack of information had failed to reveal Rommel's absence.

Derna is a pleasant coastal town, where the pace of life is, at best, pedestrian. The old covered souk is not large, but around every turn is a gem. In a whitewashed Moorish courtyard with central fountain and a dazzling backdrop of purple bougainvillaea, the tea shop was busy. People have been waiting here for years — mostly for their tea to arrive. As always, the locals preferred to talk about Premiership football rather than politics.

By June 1942, the British had fallen back from the Ghazala Line under the steady assault of Rommel's forces. His greatest victory came on June 21st when the British fortress of Tobruk fell to his panzer divisions. As the Allies retreated to El-Alamein, the whole of Egypt seemed to be at his mercy. But through July, the battles at El-Alamein marked the end of German hopes of a rapid victory, and after Montgomery's Eighth Army consolidations, the Axis forces were pushed back once again across Cyrenaica.

During the chaos of the summer of 1942, Jim was taken prisoner by the Germans. From there he was transferred to a POW camp in Italy, where he saw out the rest of the war until Italy surrendered.

My own final push towards Tobruk was on a sweltering day, and the thought of fighting a war in such conditions was incomprehensible.

The Tobruk of today bears no scars of those dramatic happenings 60 years ago. I imagined rusting tanks littering the desert and twisted wrecks in the harbour, but it has all been removed. Below the big Masirah Hotel, the large desalination plant and the massive oil refinery, the harbour is still strategically impressive, but it is impossible to conjure up visions of war in this sleepy backwater of Mediterranean trade. A pair of kingfishers flashed brilliantly across the silent mirror-like surface.

I didn't need to cross the Egyptian border to visit El-Alamain; I had been there 20 years ago on earlier travels, when I wondered what it would be like to get into Libya and whether a visit would ever be possible.

All that remained was to visit the war cemeteries. The German memorial is a stone crusader-style castle overlooking Tobruk harbour. The names of 6,026 German soldiers who died in the campaign are carved into huge black slabs set back from a central courtyard. The constant crackling of high voltage electricity cables looping just a few metres from the crenelated ramparts lends it an air of unreality.

The Tobruk War Cemetery for British and Commonwealth soldiers is a further two kilometres towards Egypt. Together with those buried at Acroma some 24km to the west, there are 8,128 souls who never returned.

It's sobering to wander around war graves and an opportunity to be grateful for the times we live in. Row upon row of neat white headstones represented not only British, ANZAC, Canadian, Sudanese, Baluchi and Rajputana Rifles, but also Polish, Czech and West African soldiers. No matter how hard you try it's impossible to imagine what these young men went through before dying in Libya.

Walking between the stones, you cannot help looking for familiar surnames and wondering if they were relations of friends. The youngest I found was 19, the eldest 40.

Jim was lucky and made it to 76. I always remember him saying, "The world is out there, you've just got to go out and make it yours."

I could now say I'd got 'out there' myself.

A first class overland experience

by Jon Ronson

I had finished writing a book. I was without cash and wanted a break. So I wrote to a safari outfit, told them I was a journalist and asked if they could possibly provide me with a free holiday? They said yes. Three weeks in Zimbabwe. First class. "Overland," they said. Whatever that meant.

This was the best possible news. I was thrilled at the prospect of sipping apéritifs in African resorts, gazing at creatures from the hotel window while dancing indigenous locals made me recognise salient truths about myself. It would be humbling, yet first class, which is the best sort of humbling.

I spoke to my outdoor-minded friends who enthusiastically recounted tales of safari virgins having to climb trees to elude oncoming rhinos and being attacked by baboons.

"Attacked?" I said. "How does one avoid this?"

"Whatever happens, don't throw the fruit back at them," they said.

"I suppose that they're as frightened of us as we are of them," I said.

"Don't be ridiculous," they said. "We're not frightened of them."

"What if there are no trees to climb?" I said.

"Run in a zig-zag," they said. "And when you're camping in the bush, keep the sleeping bag over your head."

The week before I was due to leave for Harare, the brochure arrived. I tore the envelope open. It quicky became clear the trip would not be as I had imagined it. The tents were not large and they did not have carpets hanging from the walls. They were, in fact, very small and we were expected to erect them ourselves.

The brochure included the portentous phrases; '*rising with the sun*' and '*duties include gathering wood*'. A worrying thought. Wood-gathering is not a strength of mine. The closest I got to gathering wood was purchasing a box of matches and the Sunday papers.

As I read further, I saw that the small print stated (and this was the most extraordinary thing I had ever heard): *'All our African Safaris are based on camping. Sometimes this takes place in campsites, in the bush, in the garden of a friendly villager, or in the grounds of a hotel.'*

In the grounds of a hotel? What the fuck was this? I don't book into a hotel and sleep in the garden. And if the villagers are really that friendly, what's wrong with the spare room?

And the tiny writing that said that our duties (the last time I performed a duty was when I was 12) included cleaning the vehicle. The brochure went on to state that we must enter the experience with a positive outlook, that we must be prepared to pull our weight or we become very unpopular amongst the group. And then the terrifying reality hit me with the force of an oncoming herd of rhinos — I was going to be in a group.

How would the group cope with the knowledge that I was a deficient wood-gatherer? Would they turn against me? Nobody likes a shabby wood-gatherer. Would they misinterpret it as a shortcoming?

I studied the brochure's typical group photograph for clues of what my retinue would be like. There they were, all sitting atop a Land Rover, grinning, arms outstretched. One was carrying a viola. They appeared elated: a bunch of blonde, muscled, backpackers, the men standing by piles of wood, pointing at the wood, the women oozing respect for the quality of the heap.

And I could see from the expressions on their faces that when you're in the jungle, wood counts. When you strip away all the materialism of Western living, all the lies that can be purchased with hard currency — the cars, the flat, the nightclubs, when all that counts is the gathering of wood, the calibre and volume of the mound, then you'd better gather with vigour, for there will be no escape. Not even from yourself.

On the next page was a photo of a lion standing over a bloodied cadaver of an unfortunate wildebeest, who, one assumed, had spent too much time watching TV and going to restaurants to master the precarious ways of the jungle.

Zimbabwe. One week later. Let me begin by introducing you to my group: I shall call the two Australians who sat in front of me Miss Native Healing Technique and Miss Goddess of Soil Rapture. Maybe that'll get confusing. OK, I'll call them Sturdy Dyke One and Sturdy Dyke Two. They were silent. Sturdy Dyke One would spend each day recording authentic African street noises on her tape recorder and play them back quietly to herself in the bus, while smiling serenely.

Sturdy Dyke Two would say nothing for hours, and suddenly — the moment we passed a mud hut or an exquisite sunset — yell "PHOTO STOP," leap out, and snap away a roll of film.

Sitting behind me were two teenagers going through hormonal changes. I shall call them Young Mister Hormonal Change One and Young Mister Hormonal Change Two.

Young Mister Hormonal Change One had discovered a band called Rage Against The Machine and insisted on quoting lines from their songs to illustrate whatever event occurred. Thus: we're driving through a savannah, and some baboon throws a rock at the bus, and Young Mister Hormonal Change One says; *Fuck You I Won't Do What You Tell Me/Fuck You I Won't Do What You Tell Me/Fuck You/Tell Me/Fuck You/Tell Me.*

Then there was Group Leader Stewart who knew the words to every Supertramp song. He didn't just know the words — he was also familiar with the drum patterns.

Stewart said things like; "Let's just bibble into town, and keep your wallets in your sweaty little mitts, and if you give me $5 then we're squitz."

There were others — Anna, an enthusiastic Scandinavian who was in favour of all climatic changes.

"Rain," she said. "Wind, sun, snow. They're all the same to me."

There was a German man and wife who didn't talk. I shall call the wife Steffi because that is the only female German name I can think of apart from Claudia, which was her real name. Steffi was offended by the lack of tread on my walking shoes.

"You'll fall off the rocks," she said. "You'll fall, you know. You should

have bought my brand: I am A Sanctimonious Outdoor Imbecile Shoes."
Or something like that. I'd stopped listening. I was planning my escape.

Our basic itinerary was this: drive for eight hours a day through
Zimbabwe's grassland listening to Supertramp's *Breakfast In America*.
Every so often we'd get out of the bus, climb a large mountain to look at a
ruin, and then drive 300km before parking at a lay-by-cum-rubbish-
dump. It would be dark by now, so we'd hit our thumbs with a mallet while
trying to hammer a tent peg into concrete.

Each night Stewart performed his nightly lecture, which consisted of
variations on the following themes:

1. All indigenous Zimbabwe residents are thieves, and will stop at
nothing to plunder our tent pegs and sell them on the black market for
food and cigarettes.

2. If we let the tent pegs out of our sight for a moment, we'd be held
personally responsible for their replacement cost.

3. We were all having a marvellous time, and would continue to do so.

The next morning, we would awake to discover ourselves terrifyingly
situated in the direct path of large oncoming vehicles, just three miles away
from a charming little village where comely, beaming hoteliers charge
US$10 a night for a sumptuous meal, a hot bath and a huge double bed.

We drove into more grassland, through quaint villages where, in an
energising display of hands-across-the-ocean cultural unity, the entire
community (tribal elders, beaming children, ladies with washing on their
heads) would gather at the roadside to point and chuckle at the bus.

In return, we threw sweets out the window, hitting small boys on the
head, while Stewart cranked up the engine and drove away, coating the lot
of them in a noxious haze of red dust.

We asked to stop to buy supplies, but Stewart said no. He reminded us
once again that:

1. All indigenous Zimbabwe residents are thieves, and will stop at
nothing to plunder our tent pegs and sell them on the black market for
food and cigarettes.

2. If we let the tent pegs out of our sight for a moment, we'd be held
personally responsible for their replacement cost.

3. We were having a wonderful time.

This basic schedule continued for four whole days, right through the
Botswana border, until we pitched camp in the Kalahari desert.

"Okey dokey," said Stewart. "We're home. Who's on table and stool duty tonight?"

"ME," yelled Sturdy Dyke Two.

"Jon," continued Stewart. "You're cook wallah tonight. What's going to be hot off the stove?"

"Nice toast tonight," I replied. "Nice toast with lovely butter."

I cleaned the stove. Anna asked me if I needed any help.

"Okey-dokey-hippety-hop," I replied. Then I paused and gasped. What had I just said?

And, with a start, I was hit by the ominous truth. I was turning into the Patty Hearst of African adventure holidays, my memories of fashionable London society evaporating irrevocably. I was becoming merely a thing that sleeps in tents, a thing that cooks for 15 with boundless enthusiasm.

My initial paranoia, before embarking on the trip, was that I might fall victim to Kaspar Hauser Syndrome: that I may somehow become isolated from the group in the middle of the bush, and they would find me in 15 years walking around on all fours. But now I discovered that a much more tenable fate might befall me: that I might become a full-time robust and hardy person — taking up juggling, travelling around the world and working in bars.

Boom bom bom boom bom bom boom. I turned on my torch and looked at my watch. Boom bom bom boom bom bom boom.

It was 4am. Where were those jungle drums coming from? Their noise echoed through the desert. They could have been a kilometre away or they could have been 100 metres from us.

With a start I scrambled from my sleeping bag. I was convinced my tent pegs were about to be shanghaied by vicious, scheming locals, and that the boom boom boom of the jungle drums was the call to alert their fellow tribes-people: "Boom boom. Campers. Boom boom. Nearby. Boom boom. They have tent pegs. Boom boom. Let's get the tent pegs. Boom boom. They are helpless. Boom boom. We are not. Boom boom. We must take their tent pegs."

Stewart's nightly lectures had got to me. I was fearful. I had to retrieve and bury my tent pegs. I had abandoned three or four in a bag a few metres from the tent, and the safety of my tent pegs was foremost in my mind.

So, armed with a can of insect repellent (for spraying in the bandits' eyes, should it come to it) and a rubber torch, I crept out from underneath the canvas. There was no question in my mind that the enemy were within yards, skulking through the undergrowth, eager to steal my tent pegs and get me into trouble with Stewart.

The outside world was eerily silent. Our campfire was glowing with its final dying embers. The stars were huge — far huger than they are in Britain, but more or less the same thing. It was the crack of dawn, and here I was in a field in the middle of the southern hemisphere clutching a large torch with which to bludgeon a mob of nonexistent political foe to protect what were basically, emotional attachments apart, tent pegs.

I found my tent pegs and buried them. I hurried back to my sleeping bag. Our encampment was not attacked. We were not pillaged.

The next morning we drove into the local village to purchase supplies. Stewart reminded us that indigenous Zimbabwe residents were thieves, and would stop at nothing to plunder our tent pegs and sell them on the black market for food and cigarettes. The group nodded.

We pulled up. Stewart turned off the engine. Gingerly, we crept through the gathered locals. I smiled a hello. The locals cautiously smiled back. I got talking with them. Stewart shot me an annoyed glance.

"We think you are crazy," said one young man to me. "You drive this ridiculous bus for hours on end. You sleep in the outdoors. What is this madness? Why do you pay to sleep outdoors? You pay to sleep in hotel, that we understand. But you pay to sleep outdoors? This is crazy."

"I too," I said, "think it crazy."

We shook our heads.

"Last night," I said, "we were camping a few miles away and I heard jungle drums over the horizon."

"Jungle drums?" he said. "This is a desert."

"Well," I said. "Desert drums. I don't know."

"Really?" he said, frowning. "What did they sound like?"

"Boom bom bom boom bom bom boom," I said.

There was a silence. And then, suddenly, his face brightened and he roared with laughter. He said something to his companions and they too roared with laughter.

"What?" I said. "What is it?"

"We had a disco last night," he said. "Some of our young men were coming home from the army, so we had a celebration disco. You heard the 'boom boom boom' of the disco. Abba. *Dancing Queen. We Are Family.* Sister Sledge. Those were your jungle drums."

It was Monday evening, three nights later, and I was sitting underneath Africa's largest tree with the following people: David, a middle-aged and inordinately wealthy company director from the Home Counties; his wife, Vanessa, a key member of the district's foremost golf club; Cobra, a tall and intriguingly silent Kalahari bushman who was holding a spear; and Ralph.

Ralph was raised in the desert by his white-bushman father, Ostrich Jack, who is in the *Guinness Book Of Records* for shooting 56,000 crocodiles. Jack was killed in a plane crash in 1992.

Now Ralph runs a safari operation called Jack's Camp, charging couples like David and Vanessa £500 a night to experience life in the desert.

I could no longer stand Stewart's paranoia, the brainwashing, the xenophobia, so I'd jumped ship, and I was now staying at Jack's Camp, which was beautiful and ornate and worth every penny.

Ralph is revered by the bushmen, who think he, like his father before him, can turn himself into a lion at will. Ralph and Cobra were the best-looking men I'd ever met — also, they could spot an ostrich from a mile away and live in the desert for weeks on end eating roots.

Just as I was trying desperately to think of something I could do that Ralph and Cobra could not (I've my doubts, for instance, that either of them could write a pithy column on contemporary urban mores), Home Counties Vanessa scanned the imposing desert vista and said to Ralph: "You know what you should really do with this place?"

"Hmm?" said Ralph, slowly turning his head from the fire.

"Turn it into a golf course," said Vanessa. "No, no. Give me a chance. You could just dig a few holes and put in some flags. It wouldn't even be eco-unfriendly."

There was a long silence, filled only by the crackling of the fire and the faraway call of a lilac-breasted roller bird.

"Medicine," said Cobra. "Good bird. Very good. Strong. Ha ha."

I looked up at the sky: the stars were as bright and impressive as the stars you get at the London planetarium. The sunset had been and gone, and for a while the sky looked as colourful as it does on a Roger Dean poster. I knew where I was with nature tonight, and I felt safe.

Vanessa was quiet now: she was obviously feeling a little guilty about the golf course suggestion, which hadn't gone down well.

We were sitting under a tree that is worshipped by locals as a place of great spirituality and was also a meeting point for famous colonials such as David Livingstone. It is a historic and impressive tree, so Vanessa had another go.

"Being out here," she said, "is very different from the Home Counties, and it makes one wonder about... well... very deep things."

Then Ralph spoke. He told the story of his father's crash (Ralph himself was in the plane), and how he was invited last year to witness, as one of the only white men ever, a trance-dance initiated by a tribal elder who could make his spirit fly around the world through space and time. He had never met this elder before, and the elder knew nothing about Ralph and could speak no English. After the dance had been going for an hour or two, the elder suddenly began to change his demeanour.

"I knew immediately what he was doing," said Ralph. "He was re-enacting a plane crash."

The elder acted out the crash in the most minute and awful detail — incorporating things that only Ralph knew. As he told this story, David, Vanessa and I sat in rapt attention. I had never heard a story like this before.

After Ralph had finished telling his story, nobody said anything for a long time. I could tell that David and Vanessa were profoundly moved by the occasion, and Vanessa took a deep breath.

"You know," she stammered eventually, "a very similar thing happened to a friend of mine in Surrey."

Then we headed back to the camp. In the truck, David turned to me and whispered: "You know, I work with computers and I've probably put tens of thousands of people out of jobs. Jobs that I've convinced people that computers could do better. I am conscious of that and I feel awful about it."

"Will our lives ever be the same again?" asked Vanessa.

A rabbit got caught in the headlights, and the truck bumped violently over an aardvark hole. Vanessa was knocked off her seat and on to the floor.

"But you know," she said, brushing herself down, "the food here could really be better. I've got a dicky tummy. And..." her voice lowered to a whisper "...those black people making the dinner — who knows if they even wash their hands?"

Jon Ronson THEM:
Adventures with Extremists

Is there really, as the extremists claim, a **secret room** from which a tiny elite secretly **rule the world**? And if so, can it be found? Them: Adventures with Extremists is a **romp into the heart of darkness** involving 12-foot **lizard-men**, PR-conscious Ku Klux Klansmen, Ian Paisley, **Hollywood** limousines, the legend of Ruby Ridge, Noam Chomsky, a harem of **kidnapped sex slaves**, David Icke, and Nicolae **Ceausescu's shoes**. While Jon Ronson attempts to locate the secret room, he is chased by **men in dark glasses**, unmasked as a **Jew** in the middle of a **Jihad** training camp, and witnesses CEOs and leading politicians undertake a bizarre **pagan owl ritual** in the forests of Northern California. He also learns some **alarming things** about the looking-glass world of **them** and **us**. Are the extremists right? Or has he become one of **Them**?

THEM by Jon Ronson, published April 2001, £16.00 PICADOR

'OVERLAND'

Why choose Africa? Well, learning to read with Willard Price and progressing to Wilbur Smith as a romantic start. Then such books as *The Africans* by David Lamb and *The Scramble for Africa* by Thomas Packenham.

Tales of tribal wars, the Arab slave trade, the colonial imperialists and the Cold War with the East and the West using African countries as side line battle grounds. Include then the likes of Field Marshal Idi Amin Dada VC (self awarded), Emperor for Life Bokassa of the CAR and Zaire's Mobutu (too many names to remember), who used to charter Concorde for trips to Paris.

All in all, a fascinating place. Study a bit of history and you will discover that just about every man-and-his-dog has tried to take a chunk of Africa to get rich from. Few have ever succeeded and many have made the most almighty hash of it.

Attempting to cross the Sahara and Democratic Republic of the Congo alone was not big on my list of things to do so I opted for a group, a large truck and all the canvas it could carry. Looking back it was a very wise decision. The chance to see the most incredible sites, tackle some of the worlds harshest climates and meet the friendliest people mustn't be missed — especially when it means that you can have fellow travellers to talk about your travels to, people who won't get bored and tell you to shut up. Having travelled for years, friends and family can only take about 5 minutes of "when I was in..." hence the engraved Zippo I got from fellow students — '*Mr When I was in...*'.

This brings me to my present occupation. Managing Director of Encounter Overland. What else could I do when I was offered to talk about my travels and get paid for it? I was even allowed to bring my own photo-albums. The real joy was that people would be nice

ENCOUNTERS

enough to listen and then pay to be able to copy me. I have even inherited the task of deciding whether or not we will develop new trips through the Amazon basin or conquer new corners of continents missed by my predecessors. Yes, there is paperwork but just the memory of practically urinating on the foot of a 3 ton Bull Elephant by moonlight or being called Monsieur Lambert by half of West Africa (they filmed Tarzan in Cameroon) more than makes up for that.

Sport was a big eye opener for me in Africa. I was once asked by a Ugandan which football team I supported. On replying, he politely asked me to let my fellow supporters know that we should stop all the riots and thuggish behaviour as it was drawing the game into disrepute. Little was he to know that 4 years later I was to play international rugby for his country and for Zambia all in the same day!

There is a unique draw to Africa unlike anywhere else I have visited. Somehow it implants a gene that continuously says "come back, come back".

I've managed to hold it down to just 5 visits. I still don't know anyone who has been and not returned: perhaps it's in the water? Just remember that opportunities don't come from nowhere and you have to make the most of any given situation be it to your advantage or someone else's. Take whatever comes your way.

One last tip, if you are in East Africa, you can forget your P's and Q's — just remember your T's and A's.

James Chetwode
Managing Director
Encounter Overland

NB: In Swahili, please is
Tafadhali and thank you is
Asante sana

Maverick in Madagascar

by Mark Eveleigh

This is not my own lie. This is a lie that the ancestors told me.

Intrigued by tales of the Vazimba people – a mysterious tribe of white pygmies according to some accounts; an invisible telepathic people according to others – Mark travels to the ancient 'Isle of the Moon'. Accompanied by his pack bull Jobi, he treks across Madagascar, crossing the forbidden bandit country of the 'Zone Rouge'. Before Mark comes to the end of his quest, he must learn to tell myth from reality in a land that has spawned sacred crocodiles, sorcerer-bandits, blood-guzzling spirit animals and a bizarre socialist pirate commune. Mark Eveleigh exuberantly captures the spirit of Madagascar in this magical modern-day adventure.

ISBN: 1864503297
Price: £6.99
US$12.99
Published: April 2001

189